BEING & DOING

A WORKBOOK FOR ACTORS

By ERIC MORRIS, author of NO ACTING PLEASE

A Whitehouse/Spelling Publication

International Standard Book Number: 0-8256-9922-3

Designed by John M-Röblin

Distributed by Quick Fox, 33 West 60th Street, New York 10023

ACKNOWLEDGMENTS

I would like to thank Bill Bordy, editor and owner of the *Dramalogue,* for the opportunity to write the column in his newspaper and for his help in the evolution of this book.

Thanks also to Daniel Spelling for his many creative contributions in the production of both my books, *No Acting Please* (written with Joan Hotchkis) and *Being and Doing.*

My gratitude to all the actors over the years who have taught me more than I have them.

I wish to thank Joan Adlen, a marvelous photographer, for most of the pictures in this book.

And to Joy, my wife, whose support in everything I do never waivers.

TABLE OF CONTENTS

THE CRAFT

CONTENTS

THE BUSINESS -25

PREFACE

Being and Doing is not just a title; it embodies the philosophy of an entire approach to acting. You see people busily DOING things every day of your life: pursuing their careers, talking, eating, laughing, crying, arguing, being sad and happy. What makes them do what they do? Is it arbitrary? Is it instinctive? Whatever it is, it certainly comes from impulses that stimulate the *need to do.*

My point is that in real life, our actions are the result of real impulses that cause responses expressed in action or emotion, while on the stage or in films we often see actors DOING things that seem to have no real origin. It appears that the actors' emotions are there because they are supposed to be, and for no other reason. When that happens, and it happens quite often, behavior on the stage has no organic origin and denies reality. The actor is out of touch with his own reality and is involved with the production of nonauthentic emotional expressions. This leads to presentational acting which is without dimension or spontaneity.

The work that I am involved with, and what this book is about, is called BEING. It is dedicated to the search for truth in each actor—to what he or she really feels and to the expression of that moment-to-moment reality. That is the very basis from which theatrical truth comes. The exercises in the section dealing with the instrument, and some in the section on craft, are designed to eliminate the blocks that keep the actor from feeling comfortable reaching the BEING state. Truth comes from truth, and cannot come from any other place.

While this book is in no way a complete treatise on my approach to acting, it is a good workbook that you can use to help yourself solve acting problems. The craft section explores the most important and applicable craft techniques, and these approaches are described very simply. In the business section I attempt to share some experience with the commercial end of the profession and suggest ways that you might avoid some of the pitfalls.

All the lessons are designed and constructed in small increments and can be extracted from the text and worked on for a day or more. You may skip around, using exercises from the instrumental section at the same time that you are working in craft areas. You may repeat some exercises over and over again. A number of exercises are described repeatedly in the text, and there are reasons for that. Some exercises can be used for several purposes, while others have a number of different emphases.

Have fun with the work, and feel free to involve other actors whenever possible. If you follow the format of the book, it will be very easy to establish a daily working schedule.

The lessons in this book are based on a column, "The Craft Corner," that I wrote over a three-year period for the *Dramalogue.*

Eric Morris

THE INSTRUMENT

THE INSTRUMENT

This section of the book deals with YOU, your body, your intellect, your emotions, and your voice. Just as a musician has an instrument to play, the actor's instrument is himself. That instrument must be tuned and ready to play, and that is what I refer to when I speak of instrumental preparation. We are born into a world that is inhibiting and judgmental. We develop protections and blocks that keep us from realizing our emotional potential, not to mention the ability to express ourselves freely. Those insulations block us off not only from other people, but also from ourselves. What must be done is to eliminate all the blocks and fears that hold the bulk of our creative talent inside.

If you have chosen to be an actor, you have a responsibility to stimulate and express the entire range of human emotions. The idea is not just to represent the emotions but to experience and express them! Yet after spending twenty years or more stifling your impulses, you cannot expect to step on a stage and be emotionally as free as a bird. So your first priority is to concentrate on eliminating your emotional obstacles. That is where the instrumental therapy emphasis comes in. Over the years I have developed and discovered hundreds of techniques and exercises that specifically deal with problem areas in self-expression. These techniques are designed to be used repeatedly in order to tear down the walls that have been built up over a lifetime.

BEING is the word I use to represent the goal of this kind of preparation. BEING is the behavioral state in which you are comfortable allowing yourself to feel and express all emotions impulsively, doing no more nor less than you feel. It is not just something to be desired; it is totally necessary in order to become an organic and creative actor. Mastering the craft of creating realities is dependent on you, the actor, being ready to open yourself up as a human being. If you do not, then you cannot be reached on an authentic level and your acting remains superficial.

The instrumental section is dedicated to problems, common and unique, that relate directly to YOU. Some of the exercises show you how to find your obstacles and eliminate them. You should work on the instrumental exercises in combination with the craft exercises that are described in the second section of the book. Of course you cannot simply read a book and become an actor. But if you do the work outlined on these pages and do it consistently, you will achieve the BEING state and learn how to use a craft that will put you way ahead of most other actors.

THE BEING STATE

For many years I have been working on a system of acting, based on "The Method," that I call BEING. As an actor I was constantly frustrated with Method techniques that didn't work for me, and as a result I started to ask a lot of questions. What were the obstacles that stood between me and using techniques that were supposed to work? Why did other actors have similar difficulties with these approaches? Was the Stanislavski system easier to discuss than it was to use?

I started on a journey that took the better part of twenty years. After much experimentation, and the cooperation of hundreds of my students and contemporaries, I developed an approach that is dedicated to seeking and finding the roads in to the self. It eliminates lifelong inhibitions against the acquisition of a state of BEING from which all theatrical truth can emanate. From this BEING state you can use the Method.

BEING YOU

The very best thing you have is YOU! Who you are, what you are, how you think, and the unique individuality that is YOU. There is not another one like you in the entire world. Even if you don't believe this, just for a moment suppose that it's true. If you agree that you are truly special (and you are), then what are your responsibilities to develop and use your unique qualities? What must you do to BE who you are in relation to all circumstances? Yes, you must do many things to free yourself of the restrictions that have been imposed on you since birth!

Well-meaning mothers and fathers who tell you that you should be seen and not heard, teachers who squelch you in the name of discipline and control, and religion that directs you to humble yourself and stifle normal impulses—all these agents deal in propriety, and all have had their impact on you. They robbed you of most of your impulsive expression by the time you were ten years old. You grew into adulthood with a lot of inhibitions and insecurities, and what is even more unfortunate, you grew out of touch with what you really feel.

What can you do to change these lifelong patterns? The first step is to accept the fact that *you have the right to be everything that you are.* You have a right to all your feelings, and a right to express them. When you begin to accept that, you have taken the first step on the road to BE-ING. It is not an easy road and you are going to encounter many obstacles along the way. What isn't allowed presents itself very subtly. You may encounter the disapproving glances of friends and the criticism of others who want to maintain the social status quo. It is difficult to take the first few steps, but I promise you that once you have, you will gain momentum. Pretty soon you will be running and then flying!

What does all this mean to you as an actor? It means everything! It is the difference between being a "competent" journeyman actor who does the job but is always somewhat predictable, and an artist who is never the same, whose work is always unique and exciting. How many actors do you know who fit this description of an artist? I'll bet not many—which is unfortunate, since almost everyone is capable of BEING.

How do you work toward all these wonderful things? You begin by doing your homework daily . . . you start to look for your real feelings . . . you stop accepting solidified concepts and get in touch with what's really going on inside. When someone asks you how you are, you tell them the truth instead of saying "I'm fine." You begin to deal with your lifelong habits of "social obligation." Oh yes, you have thousands of little loyalties to propriety and social expectations—like smiling when you pass someone, even when you don't feel like smiling. "That's a little thing," you say. "How can such an inconsequential action keep me from BEING?" But it can, particularly since you multiply that little automatic action by thousands. It is another moment when you have put something there that isn't your *here-and-now* truth. What is insidious is that we do so many things that we have conditioned ourselves to doing. All those things must be identified and eliminated so that we can step on the stage and allow an audience to experience our moment-to-moment realities.

All the exercises I have developed are some of the ways that you achieve BEING. You must do them every day of your life. You must make them as much conditioned reflexes as the behavior you have been taught since childhood. The best way to break bad habits is to create better ones. It isn't easy! It takes a lot of work and, most important of all, courage.

Of course you can read this and say, "Nonsense; if you've got it, you've got it! I used to take all that seriously, but no one really cares. All they want you to do is know your lines and not cost them any time, and you'll get work from them again." That is, obviously, a rationalization. Deep down where we all know ourselves, you have to admit that the truth is the truth and it will remain so no matter what you tell yourself.

Jazan doing a BEING exercise in class

ELIMINATING THE OBSTACLES TO BEING

I have spent a lot of time working on eliminating obstacles—the problems that keep you from BEING. To make things somewhat easier, here is a list of some of the exercise groups that deal most directly with the obstacles to BEING.

THE EXPURGATIVE GROUP

All the exercises in this group are large! They are designed to eliminate tension and get rid of constipated emotion. In addition, they stimulate an emotional connection with what you are feeling on a deeper level.

Yeah, Yeah!
This exercise is done by repeating the "Yeah" with great exuberance and with an accompanying physical involvement. Usually it is very exciting to both the actor and the audience.

Dump
The title describes the exercise. Very loudly, you begin to express all the conglomerated emotions that you feel—your complaints, frustrations, desires, and so on—until you have "dumped" yourself empty.

Exorcism
Also a very large commitment. Vocally and physically you push the things out of your life that disturb you. "Get away from me! I want you out of my life!" are commands you scream while using your arms in a pushing action, until you feel free of tension and more emotionally connected.

In the midst of an Excorcism exercise

"You Never Gave Me!"

THE VULNERABILITY GROUP

These exercises should get you into areas that stimulate vulnerability.

You Never Gave Me
Talking to people who are not present as if they were, you indict and accuse all the people in your life of not giving you the things that you needed. For example: "You were never there for me! You never loved me! You never gave me any support!" Take it from there.

Deathbed
This exercise can be done in two ways. Either you can talk to someone you love who is dying, or you can image that you yourself are on your deathbed. Talk to the meaningful people in your life, saying the things that you never had the chance to tell them.

MONOLOGUES

Monologue exercises help you to get in touch with all that you feel and make it available in your expression.

Imaginary Monologues
Talk to meaningful people about things that are important to you. Selectively emphasize people and topics that will make you vulnerable. Of course, you are relating to people who are not really present at this moment, but talk to them as if they were. Knowing that you are after vulnerability, creatively lead yourself into areas that you know will affect you.

Inner Monologues
There are several kinds of inner monologues: Character Inner Monologue and Impulsive Inner Monologue. The impulsive type follows a stream-of-consciousness format except that you selectively emphasize a specific object (person) to relate to. For example:

She's talking to me . . . I can't follow what she is saying, or maybe I'm not interested . . . She's pretty . . . I wonder if she's married . . . I think I'll ask her . . . I keep getting distracted by other people in the room . . . I like her, but she's a little dull . . . I wonder if she thinks I'm attractive . . . [And so forth.]

All this inner life is going on at the same time that you are talking with the person. What you do is allow the life to become an inner monologue that happens simultaneously with the conversation.

ANTIPROPRIETY GROUP

This entire area deals with the obstacles we build up over a lifetime, all the "don'ts" and "shouldn'ts." We behave as the social situation dictates, and we grow into "polite people" who stifle the real impulses we feel. We reach a point where even we don't know the truth of our feelings anymore! That may be acceptable for an accountant, but it is creative suicide for the artist. Here are a few exercises that you might try in order to crack the armor of these demons that have been with you for years.

Silly Dilly

This is a large-commitment exercise. You start doing outrageously silly things, like making faces and distortive body gestures. At the same time you scream, rant, and accompany the gestures with equally exaggerated vocal silliness. It is important to do this in front of others, since it has no therapeutic value if you are alone. The exercise generally breaks down the walls of propriety. It allows you to stretch your expression and run the risk of making a fool of yourself.

Antisocial Exercises

These exercises are done either in a classroom or with a group of friends or other actors. You express all those feelings that are less than socially acceptable—things like attractions and criticisms. "I don't care about anything but me! . . . particularly at this moment . . . I don't care what you think about me!" And go on from there. The more chances you take, the more you stand to gain from the exercise. It can also include gestures and behaviors that you would not use in public.

Ann and David doing a two-person Antisocial exercise

Irrational Tantrums

You know what a tantrum is: screaming, ranting and raving, and kicking your feet on the floor. Encourage yourself to express various kinds of irrational behavior, throwing caution to the winds. Use real things that are happening in your life, and put the emphasis on not caring if your attitude or behavior is justified or not.

Try these exercises using your intelligence and common sense. Don't do or say anything that is cruel or harmful to yourself or to others.

IMPULSIVITY GROUP

There are a number of exercises in the impulsivity area. A very good one is to encourage the free flow of your moment-to-moment impulses, expressing everything you feel, including the physical impulses.

Switch Trick

This can be done alone or with the help of a friend. Suggest a series of meaningful objects all around you; then have your friend say ''Switch'' very quickly, moving you from one object to another. Encourage large, expressive responses to all the objects you have suggested. The exercise immediately gets you out of your head and encourages you to trust the moment-to-moment feelings that are there.

Stream of Consciousness

Start by verbalizing everything you are thinking or feeling. Include all the things around you, and allow yourself to wander in any direction. Sometimes you won't even complete a thought before something else takes precedence. Go with whatever takes over. For example:

I'm sitting here . . . I hear traffic outside . . . I'm tired . . . taste the coffee . . . I'm looking at the plant on the table . . . thinking about what I have to do today . . . wish I would get an interview . . . took a deep breath . . . I'm a little anxious . . . don't know what that's all about . . . looking around the room . . . should clean this place up . . . I hear some people talking outside . . . can't hear what they're saying . . . I don't really care . . . I see the telephone . . . I wish it would ring . . . something exciting happen . . . I'm bored . . . hear my own voice . . . that movie I saw last night . . . funny . . . I feel like I should be doing something right now . . . don't know exactly what . . . I'm hungry . . . want to lose weight . . . I like the quiet . . . I like being alone . . . I don't like being alone sometimes . . . feel like lighting a cigarette . . . want to quit smoking . . . I think I'll call someone . . . who? . . . look in my telephone book . . . I think I'll shower . . . [And so on, as long as you can do the exercise.]

If you practice Stream of Consciousness often, you will get into the habit of including everything you feel. Then even when you don't verbalize it, the flow of life will underlie everything that you do express. If you are in touch with all that is going on in the framework of a scene, it will add dimension to your life onstage. It will keep you from superficial behavior and from imposing only that behavior which you think the scene calls for. It will get you into the realities that live below. It will lead to the state of BEING.

WHAT IS TALENT?

Have you ever wondered what talent is? Have you ever speculated about its origin or components? Understanding talent, and particularly the talent to act, is important in developing your own. Because of the complexity of the human instrument, I don't think that there is an adequate definition of talent. On a certain level, however, it is definable.

Talent is the ability to be affected by a great and varied number of stimuli and to express your response to those stimuli in an imaginative, colorful, and individual way.

This is a very loose definition, but it is a starting place. No one can teach or endow you with talent, and it isn't learned in an acting class. But if you do understand the importance of the connection between affectability and expression, you can embark on the journey to eliminate the obstacles that living in our society have placed in your path. We all start out with an equal chance to develop sensitivity, affectability, and expression. However, the restrictions imposed by parents and teachers who are more interested in discipline, peace, and quiet than they are in the legacy of freedom create huge blocks that often last a lifetime.

Let us suppose that most of us grow up with these obstacles and come to acting filled with fear and inhibitions. What can be done to clear the way so that the talent can flow freely and intuitively? Start with square one! Begin to train yourself in awareness and observation. Find out what affects you, and encourage your responses to all the things around you that could have an impact on you. Systematically eliminate your fears in different areas of expression.

The natural process is *stimulus—affect—response—expression*. We perceive the stimulus, we are affected by it, we respond to the way it affects us, and we express the emotional response it causes. Essentially, that is the living process. Any interference at any point in the process short-circuits the natural flow of your instrument and impedes the connection between impression and expression. Therefore your training, in part, should be dedicated to learning how to rid yourself of the conditioning that has influenced the better part of your life.

Believe it or not, most actors skip this first and most important step in their training. They learn how to read lines, move on the stage, present emotion, deal with blocking, and create characters. Thus presented, the craft of acting can be taught to almost anyone in less than six months. But the process of reaching and using the purity of your instrument is the work of a lifetime. The irony is that if you don't eliminate the obstacles that keep you from BEING, the craft is useless and will not help you to create reality on the stage. Every day, ask yourself how you feel about everything around you, and encourage the expression of those feelings.

ON TRUTH

Art comes from a base of truth and cannot be stimulated from any other place! No matter what technique an artist uses, he or she cannot create reality from any other place but reality itself. An actor's technique is employed only after the person is *prepared* to use it. This happens when the actor reaches a state of life in which he or she is experiencing everything that is felt, in which the life that is there can be expressed from moment to moment, in which the actor does no more nor less than what is felt, and can remain comfortable in that state. This is much more easily said than done, since there are numerous obstacles that keep us from the state of BEING.

Before I talk about the obstacles and how to eliminate them, let's begin with the qualities you should have in order to attain the base of truth. To be able to distinguish between what is authentic and what is not is an important quality. It involves:

The sincere desire to be real.

The courage to take chances, even in the face of ridicule or rejection.

A commitment to work on you instrument and your craft every day of your life.

Above all else, the determination to be a truth seeker.

If you don't have these qualities now, they can be developed! Certainly you must possess them in order to deal with all the demons that block the path to reality. Some of those demons are social conditioning, social obligation, fear of rejection, fear of looking foolish, fear of not being "cool," the wish to hang onto things that seem to work for you, fear of failure, the expectations of other people, the insecurity of not knowing what to expect, and the habit of being so out of touch with yourself that you don't know what is there or how to begin finding it.

The bottom line is that if you settle for anything less than everything you are, you cheat yourself and the world of your true potential. I see no alternative for you but to find out who you are, what you feel, and what the blocks are that stand in the way of the real you.

SOCIAL-ROLE MOLDS

One night I started my class with an exercise that kicked off a discussion about what acting is today and why the work we see in films is, for the most part, so commonplace and predictable. I asked the group to obligate themselves to an emotional point of view toward the actors they were working with. I told them to work for a choice that might stimulate this emotional life, and to allow, permit, and include their moment-to-moment impulses at all times. I advised them to take chances and express everything they felt, no matter how outrageous it was—to have an ''anything goes'' attitude. Everyone went to work. I saw some interesting and colorful behavior, but it was well within the framework of what is acceptable on a movie set. I had wanted much more adventurous contributions, more of the expression of underlying impulses that might be contrary to the actors' concepts of what kind of behavior should evolve.

These actors were not yet breaking out of the *social-role molds* in which we all restrict ourselves. From the time we are born, we are taught to adopt certain behaviors in certain situations. We play a social role at school in class, a different role with our classmates, another one at home with our parents. We play roles at work, at church, with romantic partners, and in countless other situations.

Eventually these social roles form a mold so solid that we become unaware of its existence. At lunch with a friend, we express interest in her conversation when in fact we are totally bored. We smile politely without even knowing that it is socially obligated behavior. At parties we fall into inane party talk because it's the thing to do.

The same phenomenon occurs when you act. You habitually fall into the mold of behaving whatever way you think is the most socially acceptable. These molds destroy impulsivity and, to a great extent, your creativity! They stop you from exploring unique innovative behavior. As a result of this limitation, you fall into the trap of conceptual leadership and premeditation. Your work becomes predictable.

So what can you do to change? Start by recognizing the molds in your daily life. Acknowledge behavior that is social and does not express your real feelings. Whenever possible, express the real impulses and break the social mold. Do this a hundred times every day until you become more comfortable BEING who you really are. In your class or workshop, take the chance to express impulses that have nothing to do with your self-image. In class allow yourself to express everything and reveal your so-called strange responses. If you remember that there is a lot at stake, it will give you the courage to explore your real impulses and express them. Think of these social role molds as a kind of prison without bars that society has sentenced you to—and make your escape!

ANTIPRIVACY

For a while now I have been doing some work in *antiprivacy,* with excellent results. First let me say that what I mean by antiprivacy is not in any way a violation of anyone's privacy! Those things that you hold *private,* and specific information that could, if revealed, harm you or anyone else, need never be exposed. But we grow up in a society that teaches you a level of privacy which leaves only "party talk" or "social talk" as a way to communicate. People are supposed to show very little of their inner impulses and feelings, and we adopt this lack of expression as a way of life. Over the years we accept, from others and ourselves, words that describe emotion rather than the emotion itself. A good actor should communicate everything that is happening inside, without having to say one word. I sometimes turn the sound off when I watch television to see if I can understand the life that is taking place. It is rare that I can.

So what do you do if you want to act? Can you push a magic button and eliminate years of environmental conditioning? No, you cannot! You must start to consciously express more and more of what you feel, at the same time trying to identify more of what you feel. There are a number of antiprivacy exercises that you can try. If you are not in a workshop that encourages this kind of preparation, do it with your friends. The results are exciting.

Double Exposure
This exercise is performed one to one, moment to moment, here and now, by talking to each other and progressively revealing more and more about yourselves. You can share one exposure or only a piece of it. One person can talk for a while and then the other can take over. The emphasis is emotional. Express your innermost feelings, needs, desires . . . After about twenty minutes you should feel a lot more open and available. This exercise is also good as a preparation for acting. Try it as a scene preparation.

I Feel
Simply, in stream-of-consciousness form, say, "I feel . . ." and fill in the blank with your moment-to-moment impulses. Continue to say, "I feel . . ." and express everything that is going on.

As with all instrumental therapy exercises, you must practice these every day. They must become part of your daily work schedule. If you work in antiprivacy areas for a period of time, you will notice an improvement in the quality of your personal relationships as well as your acting.

Elizabeth and Gayle Intimately Sharing

INDIVIDUALITY

The last lesson talked about antiprivacy and the necessity of touching your deep impulses. The entire BEING concept stands on the foundation of *individuality* . . . you! There is, however, a stigma attached to terms like "individuality" and "moment to moment." What do they really mean? The first impulse most people have when they hear the word "individuality" is, "Of course I'm an individual; I'm not you, am I?" Unfortunately, this response does not communicate the real depth of the concept. It isn't possible just to *decide* to express your innermost feelings, since the protective shields have been constructed over a long period of time. To knock them down, you must do daily work in this area. The two exercises in the last lesson, Double Exposure and I Feel . . . , are good to start with; do them as often as time allows.

There are two major steps in reaching the kernel of your individuality. The first is to find out what you feel and how you feel about everything. What is your emotional point of view about all the people and things you come into contact with? It is not enough to say "Oh, I like that," or "I have mixed feelings about her." You must explore what and how you feel on a much deeper level. What are those mixed feelings made up of, and why do you feel the way you do? Don't be lazy in your exploration! Get down into the very nucleus of the feelings you have about things.

When you feel you are doing that, take the second step and *express* those impulses. There is an intimacy about your real emotions, and that intimacy is the very thing that thrills an audience—it is a glimpse into your soul. When you reach this level of reality, you'll find it is filled with a variety of life and colors that exist only there. It is this place that is compelling and exciting to you and others. When people say, "There isn't another person on earth like him," what they are probably seeing is this intimacy being shared. It is frightening to walk on this ground in the beginning; it makes you feel naked in a world of Peeping Toms. The rewards, however, are worth the fear you feel at first. There are a number of really good exercises that can open these doors.

Intimate Sharing

This exercise is done with another person—not someone that you feel particularly comfortable with, but not a person that you feel threatened by, either. Sit comfortably and relate to each other, sharing more and more of your deep and intimate emotions. At the beginning of the exercise allow yourself to express your fears and reluctancies. Sneak up on your deeper feelings.

An example of intimate emotions exists sometimes in your personal "sense of life." Watching a television special on whales one night, I was overwhelmed with reverence for the purity of life—all life. I cried for a long time about the slaughter of whales and baby seals. I can't tell you how hurt I felt about it. Most people keep those emotions to themselves because they feel others will consider them corny or hysterical.

The reality, however, is that reverence and respect for life is at the basis of your vulnerability. Instead of hiding it or apologizing for it, you should open the doors to it for the world to see. I think that what makes an actor successful is the precious shared intimacy that we all feel somewhere deep inside, but that *he* has the courage to show.

RESPONSIBILITY AND RELAXATION

What are your responsibilities as an actor? There are many! More important than getting a good agent, having pictures taken, and waiting for the telephone to ring is your responsibility to develop your instrument and become creatively ready to work.

Painters paint, writers write, dancers dance—and most actors sit and drink coffee and talk about acting. That isn't because actors are lazy or afraid to work, but because most of them don't know what to do or how to use their time productively. *You* are not only the best thing you have . . . you are the only thing you have. Being prepared to act is ninety-five percent of acting. If you know *what* to do and *how* to do it, then you can indeed do it. Knowing what and how are the things you work at every day. Daily practice of instrumental and craft exercise work is the most successful approach.

Start dealing with your responsibility to yourself by setting aside an hour or two each day to work. Pick a time when you have the least distractions. (I have found that early in the morning or late at night are my best times to work, and the times when I feel most like working.)

Tension is the actor's greatest obstacle, because it stifles your impulses and makes it impossible to express what you really feel. Before you do any kind of work you should try to relax and eliminate tension. There are many good relaxation exercises and, after trying several, you will find the ones that work best for you. Here are a couple to start with.

Tense and Relax
Lie down on the floor. Starting with the bottoms of your feet, slowly, by degrees, tighten each part of your body. Hold the tension until you are rigid from the bottoms of your feet to the top of your head. Then, from the top of your head, start relaxing each part of your body by degrees, slowly, until you have reached the bottoms of your feet. Do the exercise two or three times. It forces your muscles to relax by tiring them. It also teaches you to recognize the varying degrees of tension in your body and helps you to deal with it when you are on the stage.

Logy
This exercise is called Logy because that is the physical state and feeling you want to achieve. Again, lie down on the floor and begin by becoming aware of your own body weight. Slowly exaggerate your weight until you feel much heavier. Test your feeling of loginess by lifting your arms and legs and letting them fall of their own weight. Do this with all parts of the body, feeling the pull of gravity on each part.

These exercises are good ones to start with. There are a number of useful relaxation exercises, and you will discover others that work for you. I have talked to some actors who use meditation as a way to relax and get ready to act.

PERSONAL INVENTORY

There is no other person on this earth like you! I cannot emphasize this enough. You are as unique as your fingerprints, and your uniqueness is what you have to sell as an actor. Unfortunately, a lot of actors imitate other actors who are successful or who are working a lot. The hope, whether conscious or not, is that by this emulation they can hook into the formula for success.

The only formula that really works, however, is to BE who you are and express that life freely and fully. The following exercises deal with penetrating to your real feelings and expressing them on a here-and-now, moment-to-moment basis. When you achieve that connection, you are readier to act—and once you are ready, then you can.

Personal Inventory I
This is a Stream of Consciousness monologue which you do semiaudibly, so that you can hear yourself talking but no one else can. Ask yourself, "How do I feel?" express your feelings, and then repeat the question. During your monologue things will interfere, interrupt, and take your attention away from the process. Include these things in the monologue. For example:

How do I feel? . . . I just cleared my throat . . . getting ready to do this exercise . . . I feel obligated to do it right . . . taking a deep breath . . . How do I feel? . . . I'm looking for things to grab onto . . . my eyes are scanning the room . . . I feel anxious . . . a little tense in the chest . . . How do I feel? . . . How do I feel? . . . [And so on.]

This exercise trains you to express everything that is going on moment by moment, alleviates mental tension, and promotes a state of BEING. Do the Personal Inventory exercise as often as you like. Naturally the more you practice it, the quicker you can utilize it in your work.

What Do I Want?

The purpose of this exercise is to find out what you want—both here and now and ultimately. Instead of asking, "How do I feel?" as in the Personal Inventory exercise, you ask "What do I want?" For example:

What do I want? . . . I want to find out what I want . . . What do I want? . . . I want to be happier than I am right now . . . I want to work more . . . I want people to respect me . . . I want to be good . . . What do I want? . . . I want not to care so much about those things . . . I want to be more relaxed . . . [And so on.]

You might do this exercise for ten or fiteen minutes at a time.

Both the Personal Inventory and the What Do I Want? exercises help you get in touch with what you really feel. From that point, you can create any kind of reality that the script demands. Remember: You can create truth only from a state of truth.

MORE ON PERSONAL INVENTORY

Most of the exercises I have suggested so far are ones that you can do at home. Of course you must be selective and practice only those that time allows; don't spread yourself too thin. A good schedule will include the daily preparations of Relaxation and Personal Inventory. Elect to do some of the others on a basis of need. If you have been working steadily, you are already noticing your growth. The emphasis of this lesson is "homework," although you can involve your friends in the process. Working with other people can be fun; besides, it elevates your tension and forces you to deal with tension and social obligation.

Personal Inventory II

Do this exercise the same way as Personal Inventory I, but add an element to it: "How do I feel? Am I expressing how I feel? If not, why not?" If the answer is "No, I'm not expressing it," then ask yourself, "What can I do to express it?" If you cannot express your feelings because they would be hurtful or would jeopardize you in some way, acknowledge that fact. Experience the impulse and choose not to express it. More often than not, however, you *can* express what you feel. As a result, you will be more colorful and interesting than if you functioned above the stream of your inner life.

If you are BEING all that you can BE, you are one of a kind!

FREEDOM FROM SOCIAL OBLIGATIONS

"I want people to like me!" So you do a lot in order to be liked; right?

Most of us are concerned with what other people think of us. It is human to want to be liked and respected. But what does it cost us? If you do what most people do, it costs a lot! Your real self (what you really think and feel) and your true personality are submerged in order to display that which is most acceptable and likable. After a lifetime of "social behavior," you lose touch with the person you really are, and the imposed personality becomes you. That is not only expensive to your personal life; it is devastating to you as an actor.

First, if you want so much to be accepted and liked, you will play it safe when you act. You will take fewer chances in expressing your real impulses for fear they might not be "good" or "right." Essentially you will behave *socially* when you act, and that is counterproductive to a moment-to-moment reality.

Secondly, as a result of suppressing your real feelings for so long, you will be out of touch with them. You won't be able to function on an organic level. If you are one of these socially obligated people and you don't want to be, what can you do to change? The first step is to be honest and admit that you do an awful lot for others. Start to become aware of the little smile and the amenities that are not honest. Notice the times when you make mundane conversation just to fill a silence. Stop pretending to be interested in someone's conversation when you aren't. Find out how much you do to ingratiate yourself with the world, and STOP IT! Don't misunderstand; the alternative to socially obligated behavior is not rudeness or insensitivity. Being a boor is not desirable, but being less than the person you really are isn't desirable either.

Take Personal Inventory many times a day, particularly in social situations. Find out how you really feel and try to express that. It isn't easy to change, and the change doesn't take place overnight. If you work at it daily, however, it will surprise you to see how much more of your inner self becomes available.

When taking Personal Inventory, make sure to express your discoveries. "How do I feel? . . . I feel uncomfortable and a little strained." You don't have to verbalize your discomfort, since it might put a damper on the situation, but you should acknowledge your discomfort to yourself and not compensate by being supercool. Continue with the Personal Inventory and use your common sense about verbalizing your feelings. After a short time you will notice a great difference in yourself, and so will your friends.

DEALING WITH THE DEMON

Start your daily work by using the preparations that deal with tension and with sensitizing yourself. Personal Inventory will make you aware of your moment-to-moment state. However, tension is elusive and moves from one part of the body to the other, sometimes very subtly. Here is an exercise that will help you chase it and eliminate it. I call it Dealing with the Demon. I'm sure you must have experienced that moment on the stage or in front of the camera when you think you are ready to work—and suddenly you feel the icy clutch of tension climbing up your back and seizing your neck in its deathlike grip. At that moment it seems too late to do anything about it, so you forge ahead and work the best way you can. But you don't really have to tolerate tension; there's something you can do about it.

Dealing with the Demon
Tension is one of the ''original demons.'' Working with actors in the classroom and in commercial situations, I discovered a lot about how tension operates. Once you identify it verbally and acknowledge what it is doing to you at that moment, it will move to another place.

For example, you might feel the tight grip of tension in your chest, so you identify it and acknowledge it. Suddenly it will jump down into your legs to hide from you. Once when I was acting in a film, I'd done all my preparation and felt relaxed and related to the actress I was working with. When they called ''action!'' I was ready to do the scene. Two lines later the demon put his hand on the back of my neck, and my whole head started to shake.

I invented this exercise to train actors to hunt the demon. The enemy of tension is *exposure!* If you allow tension to stay hidden, it compounds itself. But if you expose it to yourself, you no longer have the need to be better off than you really are. You know you're tense, and instead of ignoring it, you turn to the business of getting rid of it.

To do the exercise, start a Stream of Consciousness monologue in order to stimulate a moment-to-moment flow of reality. Verbally—out loud or semiaudibly—chase your demon as it scurries through your body. For example:

Oh, I feel tension in the back of my neck. Hello there, demon. Oh, it just moved down to my shoulder. It's in my right shoulder. I know you're there. That's funny; I just became aware that my stomach is a little jumpy. It's down there now. It's in both my shoulder and stomach. I'm looking around the set; I see everybody working. Who's that the director is talking to? Oh, oh, I just felt it creep into my back . . . Hello, demon . . . I know exactly where you are, and I accept your presence! I'm not afraid of you! My throat is closing up a bit. I'm taking a deep breath, and it's okay! I know you're there. I know all the places you are and I'm going to allow you to be there—because I can't deny you.

By continuing this Stream of Consciousness exercise, you will chase your demon around your body until it loses its grip on you completely.

As with all exercises, this one depends on practice and repetition. It is an instrumental exercise, and you should do it before you work in any craft area. Don't delude yourself into thinking that you need not work every day of your life on your instrument and craft. The stigma of the classroom as opposed to the "profession" is just a rationalization that keeps actors from what they must do in order to create art.

DEVELOPING AN EMOTIONAL POINT OF VIEW

"How do you feel about that?" . . . "What do you think of him?" . . . "What's your opinion of the way the President handled that situation?" . . . These are the kinds of questions we hear hundreds of times a day, and we usually respond by offering our opinions or feelings.

But do you know how you *really* feel about things? We all know what we feel generally, but that is not what I mean. Do you know how you feel about things in depth? Most people don't. One night in class I asked the group how they felt about a current news event with major historical significance. I received only vague responses: "Oh, I think that's great," or "I didn't really pay much attention to it!"

When I speak of developing your individuality, the unique qualities that are only you, it means knowing what and how you feel about most things. *Having an emotional point of view* and being able to express that point of view emotionally is part of an actor's responsibility.

Try an experiment with a friend. Ask your friend how he or she feels about a particular subject, and don't settle for the first response. Continue to pursue your friend's feelings on the same subject. For example:

> "How did you like the film?"
> "I thought it was pretty good."
> "Yes, but how did you feel about it?"
> "I liked a lot of it, but I thought that it dragged in spots."
> "Where did you think it dragged?"
> "The love scenes seemed dull and self-conscious, and all the exposition at the beginning."
> "What was your emotional response to it, overall?"
> "Well, I felt moved by the story; it made me feel hopeful!"

Thus instead of settling for "I thought it was pretty good," you made your friend think, dig for responses, and focus on his emotional point of view. You both found out more about his response to the film, and you shared something as a result of your questioning. Do this experiment many times with several people and see what happens.

As an actor you should find a way to be interested in most things, since you deal in a variety of areas when you act. In particular, you should have an emotional point of view, know it, and express it impulsively. When you are in touch with your feelings about most things, they are available for an audience to experience, even if you say nothing.

Taking Your Own Emotional Point of View
Do this through Personal Inventory, asking, "How do I feel?" and responding to the question. Then add, "How do I feel about that?" and continue asking yourself more complex questions on the subject: "How do I feel about her? . . . I like her . . . What else do I feel about her? . . . I think she is bright . . . What do I feel about her intelligence? . . . I feel warm . . . Am I excited when I think of seeing her? . . . Yes! definitely!"

Taking your emotional temperature is a process to be done fifty or a hundred times a day. DO IT!

PREPARATION

To create reality on the stage or in front of the camera, you must start from a real place. *How* and *what* you really feel is that real place. That makes sense and sounds simple, doesn't it? Well, it isn't simple! It takes understanding of what really BEING YOU means and how to achieve that state. Most actors learn to deliver what is expected of them, and all too often this means assuming attitudes and behavior without really creating an authentic level of life. The obligation to give "them" what they want and to be good becomes a trap for many potentially fine actors. The more an actor imposes life, instead of creating reality, the harder it gets to break the habit.

Fortunately, you can begin to learn techniques for eliminating obstacles to the creative process. One way to utilize your time well is to find a good place to train. There are many able teachers around. A lot of "professional" actors feel that if you're still going to class, it means that you're not ready for professional work. That's nonsense! If you are a serious artist you can look forward to spending the rest of your life in and out of classes. You never stop growing, and there is never a time in your life when you do not have room to grow.

In addition to formal training, the most important involvement is daily practice. If you can get up each morning and approach your practice as if you're going to a job that's a joy, half the battle is over. Every morning set up something to do. For example, do some Sense Memory work over breakfast (work sensorially with your coffee, as described on pages 85 to 89) or do some Personal Inventory work so you can start the day by finding out how you feel. Later in the day you might work with the obligations of a piece of material, breaking it down and trying to fulfill small areas. Whatever you set for yourself, each day should begin with the moment-to-moment life that is happening right now.

Before you start working on anything, ''get ready to get ready.'' Prepare by doing relaxation and other exercises that make you more available and ready to work. For years I have opened my classes with a group of exercises that offer well-balanced practice in many of the preparatory obligations: Relaxation exercises, Personal Inventory, and Sensitizing. Since you already know something about the first two, let's talk about the third.

Sensitizing

This exercise should be practiced daily; it's an essential element of the actor's preparation. It enormously heightens your sensory availability. It can be performed in any position and requires that you isolate the senses.

Start with the *tactile sense,* or feeling. Beginning with the top of your head (your scalp), concentrate your entire involvement there. It's as if you are *living* in your scalp. When your scalp begins to tingle, or you feel a pulse or the heat of your body there, it's an indication that your scalp is sensitizing. Then progress to your forehead, your face, your chin, and so on, moving down your body in four-inch sections until you get to the soles of your feet. ''Live'' in each section until you feel that it is sensitized.

Next go to your *ears.* Without touching them, become aware of their structure. Then, as you did in the tactile area, live in your ears. Listen to every sound, from the most obvious to the most subtle. Become aware of their origins and directional sources all the way down to the component parts of silence. Try to become one gigantic ear or hearing device.

Then go to your *nose.* Become aware of its structure without touching it: the apertures, the inner nose, and the mucous membrane. Live in your nose. Become aware of all the odors around you. Try to smell all of them and the elements of each one. Function as if you are a giant nose.

Move on to your *mouth.* Focus on the gums, the teeth, the tongue, the cheeks. Taste the tastes in your mouth. You may taste some toothpaste left over from brushing your teeth. You may have a coffee taste, or the aftertaste of a sandwich. Do it until you even taste your own flesh.

You can sensitize your *eyes* in two ways. Visually isolate a small area—maybe the corner of a tabletop—and by living in your eyes, attempt to see every minute detail. Or look at a small portion of an object, then look away and try to visualize that portion. Look back at the object and go to another portion. Repeat the same process, living in your eyes.

The entire exercise might take fifteen or twenty minutes when you first do it, but as you practice over a period of time, you condition your senses to respond instantly, and you can run through it in less than two minutes.

If you do Relaxation, Personal Inventory, and Sensitizing exercises each day, and always before you work, they will enable you to use your instrument on a much more organic level.

MORE ON PREPARATION

Preparation is the largest component of acting and an integral part of the Method. Although the Method has as many interpretations as it has teachers, basically it is a system for creating realities onstage. If you see a person in life pretending to feel something or just mimicking life, you don't believe him, do you? It's the same in a film or play: if the actor is not truly experiencing the real life of the character in the scene, you don't accept it as reality. The Method uses techniques that help you to stimulate or pique real emotions. In order to create a true emotional life that parallels the life in the scene, you must prepare your instrument to be available to the stimuli that promote the scene's reality. In addition to preparation, you must have craftsmanship and believe in a reality-based approach to acting.

Relaxation, Sensitizing, and Personal Inventory each deals with a different part of the instrument. They are basic tools for "getting ready to get ready." Once you have done them and are readier to begin working, you must choose the right preparation for the circumstance.

First, find out where you are at this moment—how you feel—and what obstacles are present. Suppose that you have finished the three basic preparations and you find that you are still not very vulnerable—not open to reality. In that case you must choose to do something that elevates your accessibility. You can create something sensorially that really affects you and stimulates vulnerability. Or suppose that you are feeling insecure; then you may decide to work in ego-building areas. Whatever your state is, you must acknowledge it and choose the correct preparation to deal with it.

The second step is to identify your obligations to the material. Know exactly what it is that you want to feel, and select a preparation that creates the foundation for exploring the choices you will use in the scene. It is amazing how easily you can fulfill the material when your instrument is primed to work.

Up to this point I've been talking about specific preparations for getting ready to deal with material. There are other kinds of preparations that later lessons will describe: instrumental, craft, and daily-living preparations. Before you do anything as an actor, you should find out what your goals are, what kind of actor you want to be, and what approach most suits you. Of course, there are actors who say their lines, take their money, and run. If they are happy with that, they needn't concern themselves with any kind of preparation.

THE IMPRESSIVE AND THE EXPRESSIVE

I teach craft workshops regularly in Los Angeles, San Francisco, and New York. They consist of five-hour sessions of intense craft concentration. We spend all our time dealing with preparation, sense memory, and the usage of sensory work in a material framework. We explore choices, choice approaches, and the means of discovering choices. Choices are those objects which you create to stimulate the desired life. Choice approaches are the various methods by which you work to create the choice. Choices and choice approaches are described in detail on pages 117 to 120. Afterward I have regular classes with the same people, and their work is always much more specific and shows a better understanding of craft usage. For if you work with the craft, even over short periods of time, it will enable you to function with greater facility.

At the craft workshop I purposely separate the craft from the instrumental area for emphasis. In my system the actor's instrument is divided into two general categories: the *impressive* and the *expressive.* The impressive area deals with everything that comes in, or everything that the actor is affected by. The expressive area relates to everything expressive: all the emotion that the actor feels and the process of expressing that emotion. Most actors have problems in both areas, but people differ and some actors have more obstacles in one area than the other. The BEING approach strives to eliminate the obstacles in both areas. For since you can only create truth on the stage from a basis of truth, you must get to know how you really feel and what real-life impulses you are experiencing.

Taking Personal Inventory on a regular basis will put you in touch with what is going on inside you. However, knowledge of your real impulses won't always enable you to express what you know you feel. Having developed behavior that has "worked" for you for many years, you will sometimes find it impossible to activate the expression of what you are experiencing. In that case you must identify the obstacle that stands in the way.

For the actor, not having a direct passage between the impressive and the expressive amounts to artistic suicide. What can you do to start changing things? Make the decision that you want to change! When you take Personal Inventory and discover that you feel something other than what you have been expressing, compel yourself to take the chance and express what is really going on. As you do this more and more, you will build courage. Pretty soon you will be surprised to find that you are increasingly in touch with reality. It is impossible to expect unpredictable, organic life from any other source than reality.

All this is a cumulative process. The more you succeed in defeating your demons, the more able you are to BE. As you express more of your internal life, you also become more impressively affectable and balanced between the impressive and expressive.

FINDING AND ELIMINATING THE PROBLEMS

Knowing the theory and even understanding the mechanics of craft is not enough. Many times actors have struggled to tell me what they have been working for, only to become buried in generalities. When I demand that they be specific, they can't, even though some of them have an understanding of the work and how to apply it. So what's the problem? Usually it is simply a lack of discipline in being specific.

I always ask three questions when an actor completes a piece of work: *What did you work for? How did you work for it? Why did you work that way?* If the actor has difficulty answering any of them, it's usually because he or she doesn't really know. If you know what to do and how to do it, then you can do it! However, you must solidify this knowledge by daily practice and application.

An actor is an actor twenty-four hours a day, and he should be open to everything all the time. I've heard actors say, "Things like that don't interest me," or "People like that turn me off!" Everything should hold some interest for actors, since they are students of all human behavior. You never know when some little observation or insight will pay off in a future role. You are at work all the time!

DAILY WORK SCHEDULE

In this lesson, concentrate specifically on the identification of instrumental problems and some of the exercises and techniques to eliminate them.

Personal Inventory

Since Personal Inventory is the foundation of the exploration of self on a moment-to-moment basis, do it many times a day. Refer to the earlier lesson on Personal Inventory for a specific breakdown of how it works. Be sure that you express all the impulses that you discover in the exercise. Include all the distractions and preoccupations. Do it out loud or semiaudibly.

If you practice Personal Inventory intensively, it will accomplish several things for you: First, it will put you in touch with what you are really feeling. Secondly, it will encourage the expression of life that you might have been suppressing. Thirdly, it will make you aware of any inhibitions or other personal obstacles that exist and stand in the way of BEING. For example, suppose that you are feeling angry and have been sitting on it for a while. Personal Inventory will make you aware of the anger and, by allowing you to express it, will free you to experience all the other emotional life locked up with the anger. In a sense, the anger acts like a steel door that imprisons all the impulses you feel. In order to stimulate true, organic expression, you must start from a basis of reality (BEING). If you bottle up the anger, all doors to creativity are locked. Personal Inventory helps you to discover the areas you need work in.

Once you have located the problem, you must decide on an exercise to free you of it. If, for example, you are constipated with emotion as the result of suppressing your anger, then you might elect to do a Dump exercise.

Dump

This is another exercise with many applications. As explained in an earlier lesson, you do it by making big, forceful statements. Expurgate all the emotion you have locked up, until you are "empty." For example: "I'm angry! . . . I feel angry . . . I'm tired of the crap in my life . . . I want the things that I want! . . . I'm frustrated and I hate feeling this way!" And on and on, until your emotions are flowing out with no obstructions. The Dump exercise, which is one of the expurgative group, never fails to unclog the emotions. It works like dynamite on a severe log jam.

Other expurgative exercises include Abandonment (page 45), Exorcism, and Tantrums. Identify the block and choose an exercise to eliminate it, and if that exercise doesn't work, try another one.

INSTRUMENTAL PREPARATION

In terms of your responsibility, being prepared to act is ninety-five percent of acting. What kinds of techniques does preparation encompass? The kinds and number of exercises available are endless, but what is more important than having a lot of preparatory exercises is knowing yourself, your unique instrumental needs, and the procedures that will make you ready to function organically. Again, let me remind you that the two major parts of preparation are the instrumental and the craft areas. You must always deal with your instrumental problems first. Those problems range from tension to self-consciousness to a whole list of personal obstacles, any one of which can stop you from functioning.

How do you find out what is happening and what to do to help yourself to get ready? The process of work is a daily involvement in which you will become more and more familiar with your problems. By experimenting with some of the therapy exercises that I have suggested, you will find the right ones to eliminate specific individual obstacles. Below is a list of relaxation exercises that deal with instrumental problems.

RELAXATION EXERCISES

Rag Doll
This exercise is done in a standing position, arms at your sides. Start by bowing your head as if there were a huge weight on the top pulling you down toward the floor. Continue to drop toward the floor very slowly, one vertebra at a time, until you reach the point where you must bend your legs. Bend the knees and continue to move toward the ground very slowly, encouraging limpness throughout the whole body. When you have reached the floor, gently crumble into a heap. Be careful not to fall hard at this point, since you might hurt yourself or tense up, undoing all the relaxation you have accomplished.

Logy
Here is a relaxation exercise described earlier. Lie on the floor and make yourself feel heavier and heavier. Encourage the Logy state by making heavy, slothlike sounds. As you succeed at this exercise, it will become harder and harder to move and your relaxation will grow.

Weight and Gravity

Here is another weight exaggeration exercise, again performed by lying on your back. Start by becoming aware of your own weight, and slowly exaggerate this weight until it becomes a real effort to lift your arms and legs off the ground. In so doing you force the muscles to give up the tension they are holding.

Deep Breathing

Lie down and slowly begin to breathe deeply . . . deeply, as if your entire body were hollow and the air you took in would eventually reach the soles of your feet. Do the exercise until you feel relaxed enough to go on.

INVOLVEMENT EXERCISES

After you have dealt with tension, you may want to do some involvement exercises, such as Observe, Wonder, and Perceive. The purpose of these exercises is to get you out of yourself and related to people or objects that will stimulate emotional life.

Observe, Wonder, and Perceive

Encourage yourself to wonder about objects and people around you, observing elements of each object that you have never seen before or that interest you particularly. For a more complete description of this exercise, see pages 49 to 50.

In addition to relaxation and involvement exercises, your daily workout might also include some of the vulnerability exercises described in an earlier lesson.

DEVELOPING YOUR IMAGINATION

Talent has many components, including sensitivity, affectability, the power of expressing emotions colorfully, and *imagination*. The development of the ability to act is based on exercising the talent components in much the way that you work and exercise your muscles. If you don't exercise, they get flabby and undependable.

Developing and practicing with your imagination is an instrumental involvement. Do exercises every day that stimulate and challenge the imagination. You've all seen actors who start out with a great deal of promise but seem to level off into predictable work after a few years. One of the major reasons is that they stop working on their instrument and craft. The imagination is particularly important because most of your creative choices emanate from it. If you have an active and fertile imagination, your creative exploration will be exciting and unique. There are a number of good exercises that you can practice each day.

Make Up Stories

Tell yourself a story about people you see around you. Suppose you are having lunch and see a couple chatting over a sandwich. Make up a scenario about their lives: "Those two are meeting secretly because he's married and can't see her publicly . . . This restaurant is their special rendezvous . . . They've been coming here for years . . . They are very much in love, but he can't leave his wife . . ." This example is a cliche, but you can start equally simply and become more and more bizarre and adventurous. For example, you can take the same couple and assume that the man, who is an alien here to do research, has mind-controlling power. Only you and the woman can see him; the waiter doesn't know he's there . . . and so on.

Story Telling

Do this exercise with two or more people. One of you starts a story, and the other person soon picks it up and takes it in another direction. Continue to switch back and forth, weaving outrageous twists to each other's stories. It is a great deal of fun and marvelous for the imagination.

The Word Game

This is a particularly good exercise for two people—for example, you and another actor who are getting ready to do a scene, or you and a friend who are simply sitting at a table and sipping wine. One of you says a word, any word, that comes to mind—say, "circus." The other person begins to tell a story involving that word. The story does not have to be about a circus, it must only use the word. The word "circus" must become an integral part of the story; you cannot just arbitrarily drop it into a sentence. When the story is finished, the person who told it gives a word to the other person, and so on, until much time passes and the muscles of your imagination grow tired.

The Must Game

This is a game all children play, and for many years it was an exciting part of my life. Every day after school a friend and I would pretend that we were great generals or notorious figures from the Old West. For example, we would say, "I must be a very important movie star, and you come to me for advice," . . . "I must be fighting in a foxhole, and you must be the enemy," . . . "I must be . . ." "You must be . . ." and we were off and running. The success of this exercise depends on how much of a commitment you make to playing and pretending. As we grow up we develop all kinds of resistance to playing, but children are not embarrassed by the fun they have. Actors are children, and they had better be! Exercising the imagination will help to lure that child out of hiding and make you a better actor.

GETTING TO YOUR VULNERABILITY

Suppose that your greatest desire has always been to act, but that you grew up in an atmosphere of conservatism and restricted emotion. If you are male, perhaps your father called you a sissy for crying and told you that only girls cry. From your earliest memories your vulnerability was discouraged, and when you could not stifle your emotions, you were ridiculed for expressing them. Time passed; you graduated from college and decided to go to New York or Hollywood to pursue your lifelong dream, only to discover that twenty-odd years of conditioning had crippled you emotionally.

What do you do, if you still want to be an actor? You can accept the fact that you are not vulnerable or accessible and begin to learn how to fake and facilitate emotion. This is a widely accepted alternative in our profession. Or you can decide to undo the damage your family and teachers have done to you. The second is the more difficult but also the more rewarding course.

Where do you begin to strip away the insulation that took years to construct? Find a teacher who deals with those kinds of problems and commit yourself to working in the teacher's class for a prolonged period. It took you some twenty years to build your defenses, so it will take a little while to tear them down. Make the decision that you really want to be vulnerable, that you want to feel all the emotions that human beings can feel. Begin to encourage your sympathetic responses to other people. If you have an impulse to cry in the movies, encourage it; don't hide your feelings behind a box of popcorn. Emotion is beautiful!

Start doing Personal Inventory to discover how you really feel, particularly when you begin to sense the first flush of any emotion. For a little while, push your feelings out . . . exaggerate them! When it is possible, scream and yell and make very large sounds. Express your dissatisfactions loudly. After these big expurgations, you will notice a flow of emotion. Encourage it!

After a time, you can begin to do vulnerability exercises. There are a number of really good ones. Take an inventory to find the things that could or do affect you. For example, you have always felt a great deal for your mother. You might have an imaginary monologue with her, expressing all the feelings you have that you could never allow yourself to expose because they made you too vulnerable. Imagine her as being sad; imagine her saying things to you that you have always wanted to hear. Or you can imagine that other people you love are sick or dead. All these exercises are designed to have a strong effect on you so that they will stimulate your vulnerability. As you work, you will become more and more affectable. In time you will destroy the anticreative conditioning you grew up with.

FEAR

One of the "biggies" of instrumental problems is *fear*. You would be surprised how many actors—successful ones, too—suffer from creeping terror on the first day of shooting and sometimes far beyond it. Most actors learn to disguise their fear in some way, but you can be sure that it lurks just under the surface. The real problem is not the fear, but the mistaken idea that it is a bad thing and should be hidden from the director, the crew, and your fellow actors. Fear is supposed to be a mark of amateurism or a disease of insecurity that you should have gotten rid of long before you became a pro. In actuality, it is symptomatic of actors who care about what they do and who want to be good.

Everyone is afraid! Start with that assumption, because it is very close to the whole truth. Ventilate your fear; *don't* suppress it. Acknowledge it, expose it to the light of day, and accept its existence. Then, as a second antidote, become "selflessly" involved in your process. The enemy to tension and fear is involvement.

To be able to work creatively, you must put your energies into your choices and choice approaches. If that time and effort are being used to cover fear and impose compensational behavior, there are two countercreative results: First, the time you use to compensate could be used to a better end. Secondly, when you impose behavior, you stifle all the real impulses inside you. Consequently you are able to act only "from the neck up." Fear makes us do strange things, such as misusing rehearsal time in trying to please the producer and director. Rehearsal time is supposedly designed for exploration and experimentation to build the performance, but so few actors are willing to fail during this period that the "performance" starts with the first second of rehearsal. That is usually where it ends, too. You must risk the opinions of others if you are ever to use your instrument and craft properly. This whole thing is for you, isn't it? If it becomes an involvement to please others and gain their acceptance, you are going to be unhappy and frustrated.

Start with "I'm afraid, and its okay to be afraid." From that place, deal with your fear; embrace it because it is part of the whole system that makes you sensitive, affectable, and talented. If you deny one emotion, you deny others too. Whenever you feel your fear pushing you to do ingratiating things, ask yourself what you really feel and express that instead. I would rather be responded to as the person I actually am than have someone say, "He's a nice guy." Isn't this the one and only life that we are sure of? Why not live it as we should?

An Observe, Wonder, and Perceive exercise in progress

MORE ON FEAR

Besides the fact that fear is extremely uncomfortable, it is, if undealt with, destructive to creativity. Fear makes the actor do many things that block the flow of impulses, and when that natural impulsive flow is interfered with, truth is short-circuited.

Most actors are terrified that their fear will be detected, so they manufacture complex defense systems of compensatory behavior that appears relaxed and confident. It takes three times the energy that eliminating the fear would require.

How do you deal with this "demon"? First, understand that fear comes from having something at stake. You want to be good and you are afraid you might not be. Most people who are afraid *care* about their work. It is very important to know and admit your fears, and equally important to know their origin.

Once you understand the fear, you can set out to remedy the situation. If your fear comes from the insecurity of process, then you must learn more about your instrument and the craft of acting. If it comes from being obligated to be good in a role, there are numerous techniques that provide antidotes to obligation. If you care so much that it cripples you, then you must take that love for your art and put it into the process. Here are a couple of good exercises that help to eliminate tension and fear.

Deductive Observation
As in other observation exercises, watch people (or other objects) and deduce what they do, what their priorities, awareness, and involvements are, what their position in society is, and so on. By the way people dress, you can often tell what kind of work they do and if they are affluent or not. By the way they relate to their surroundings, you can see how expressive or inhibited they are. Body language often tells us how secure people feel. The way people relate to objects also says a lot. Deductive Observation is absorbing and fun, but most of all, it creates a state of selfless involvement that eliminates tension and fear. If you practice the exercise even when you are not fearful, then you will be able to do it when you are under pressure.

Observe, Wonder, and Perceive
This is a great way to get out of yourself. Simply *observe, wonder* about, and *perceive* the interesting people and objects in the immediate area. For example: "That's a pretty lady over there . . . I wonder if she's waiting to meet someone . . . She's all dressed up and has a portfolio . . . She might be an actress or a model . . . I perceive that she is fidgety; she's probably anxious or impatient . . ." You can use this technique in relation to anything. It works wonderfully!

THERAPY EXERCISES

Therapy exercises are individually designed to deal with and eliminate the emotional obstacles of each actor. In my classes the exercises I ask people to do are usually those that are the most difficult for them to do. The theory is that if you tackle the most difficult things first, you won't have to waste precious time working up to them through the easier things. This theory has been proved right over the years. Once an actor conquers a block, dozens of other emotional wellsprings open up and become usable to him on the stage. We systematically eliminate the obstacles until the actor can achieve a true BEING state, rich with all the emotional colors of the rainbow.

Suppose that an actor is shy and so soft-spoken that he or she is usually hard to hear onstage. Of course, these symptoms relate to a tension problem, and the tension must be dealt with. A good therapy exercise would be in large-commitment areas like yelling, shouting, Dump exercises, and Abandonment exercises (described in the following lesson). Large ego-expression groups like Superman (see page 57) are also helpful for shyness. When actors suffer from the "nice guy" syndrome, I have them do Antisocial exercises where they have to be nasty and rude. If someone is embarrassed by large emotions (you would be surprised at how many actors are emotionally phobic), we do vulnerability work and deal with stimuli that elicit large emotional responses.

Whatever the problem areas, there are therapeutic exercises that ultimately make the actor much more accepting of his right to experience and express those emotional impulses. What you can do at home is to take inventory, become more aware of your own obstacle areas, and design therapy exercises for yourself. If you understand the theory and you are fairly intelligent, you can come up with some good antidotes to your own problems.

As you do your daily work, be aware of the blocks you encounter. When you are in a "spot," or pressure situation, take note of the problems and start dealing with them. If you do an exercise that will help you to overcome a problem, make sure you understand that it requires repetition; miracles are very rare these days.

SOME BASIC THERAPY EXERCISES

The therapy exercises listed below are designed to eliminate instrumental obstacles and help you in craft areas. The best way to discover exactly what you need to work on is to take a Personal Inventory. Find out how you feel and what is blocking your impulsive expression. When you select your therapy exercises, work with them at home every day.

Sense Memory with Affecting Choice

Choose a person, a place, an inanimate object that affects you strongly. By asking questions about the object and answering them with the senses, you create the object until it becomes a reality. Encourage the expression of everything you feel as you work. Sense Memory is described more fully in a later section.

Imaginary Monologues with Important People in Your Life

Talk to people who are really meaningful to you: your mother, your father, old girlfriend, a close friend, or someone else. Address them *as if they were in the room* and talk about meaningful things. As you do the monologue you will become increasingly vulnerable, and it is important to express those emotions because they are affecting in themselves.

Evocative Words

Say words to yourself that relate to a meaningful experience, and continue the words until the experience again affects you. Go from one meaningful experience to another. You can say single words or short phrases. This exercise is easy to do and achieves great results.

I Feel

A very good vulnerability exercise is simply to express your own vulnerable feelings. Start by saying, "I feel . . . needful . . . I feel hurt . . . I feel alone . . . lonely . . ." [And so on.]

LARGE-COMMITMENT EXERCISES

There are many large-commitment exercises designed to free the actor from crippling problems: tension, fear, social conditioning, suppression, and constipated emotion, to name a few.

Abandonment

Making very large sounds and movements, throw your body all over the place, yelling and screaming with Abandonment. Make sure that the commitment has no form or intellectual control. When done properly it resembles someone having a "tantrum" or "fit." Carry on like this for two or three minutes. You will be amazed at the results. I have seen actors so tense that they literally could not remember their names, and after doing the exercise they began to function well.

Anger and Rage Exploration

Start arbitrarily by yelling, "I'm angry! I'm *angry!* I'm ANGRY!" Each time you say the words, enlarge the expression—until you feel yourself making the connection with your real anger. When you are in the grasp of that authentic emotion, include the subject of your anger: "I'm angry at the way you treat me! . . . I'm angry that I'm not working!" This is a good exercise for actors who fear what other people think of them, since it breaks down social obligation and fear of rejection.

Dump

Eruptively Dump all that is happening inside you, emphasizing your angers and frustrations. In a very large voice say, "I'm tired of not getting what I need! . . . I hate being tense like this . . . I won't do anything I don't want to do! . . . No, No, No . . . Nobody tells me how to live my life . . ." Go on until it is all "dumped." The Dump exercise is great for eliminating tension and getting rid of built-up frustrations. It creates an expressive flow and helps you prepare to act.

Remember to use your discretion and common sense when you do these exercises. Perform them in the proper environment where there will be no consequences from what you do and say. The work is for you, and shouldn't be worn like a badge. Try the exercises at home, in your acting class, or before you go onstage.

David doing an Abandonment exercise

MORE DEALING WITH THE DEMON

Tension is the manifestation of unexpressed impulses, and once you eliminate it, those impulses are free to flow. It is their flow that makes you colorful and unpredictable on the stage. Therefore it is extremely important to have many techniques to eliminate tension. After you have dealt with most of the crippling physical manifestations of tension, the next step is to become involved in something outside yourself. Here are several good involvement exercises that you can try.

INVOLVEMENT EXERCISES

Threshold of Interest
Look around the room and let your eyes pick out the objects that they find interesting. Stop at anything that piques your curiosity. Once you find something that is really meaningful to you, ask questions about it. For example, when you see a painting that you like, ask yourself, "Where did it come from? How old is it? Is it a print or an oil? Who was the artist? What is the subject? How many different things do I see in it?" After you have explored that object, continue to ask questions about all the things that interest you. If you do this exercise for about ten minutes, tension will completely disappear. Your focus will be away from yourself, and you will be much readier to start working.

In practicing involvement exercises, be wary of forcing involvement, since that in itself might create more tension than it eliminates. A good way to gauge an involvement exercise is to find your own level of real interest. Try it with this exercise:

Selfless Involvement

Using the Threshold of Interest as a starting point, explore, wonder at, and investigate an object without relating it back to yourself at all. Here's an example: Observing another person, you could begin wondering about his life, what he does for a living, how old he is, how he relates to the environment, and so on. Be sure that you keep the exercise objective; don't relate your involvements back to yourself. You can selflessly involve yourself in anything: people, animals, inanimate objects of all kinds, sounds, the weather—you name it.

If you work on a scene, Selfless Involvement is a good preparation before you begin to deal with the material. Start to explore the other actor, look for what interests you, and begin to wonder. If you do it silently, you won't interfere with the other actor and no one will know what you are doing.

The purpose of both these exercises is to take your attention away from yourself, and as a bonus, to stimulate a moment-to-moment life which is filled with colors and changes. Think of your daily practice as a process of establishing creative habits that will serve you well all your life.

SCARY FEEDBACK

Often my class does an exercise in which everyone asks another person for feedback—specific responses to questions like

> What do you think of me generally? . . . How do I affect you? . . . What is or was your first impression of me? . . . I've been told that I come across as aloof; do you experience me that way? . . . Do you like the way I dress? . . . Do you think that I express all I feel? . . . Do you think I'm an open person?

My students ask for feedback from at least three different classmates so that they can get a cross section of responses. If you hear similar things from several people, then you can assume that there is reason to check into these areas.

Oddly, most people are surprised by the feedback they receive. Most feel that there seems to be a great dichotomy between what they feel "inside" and how they are perceived. They find it hard to believe that their inner lives remain hidden from others. "But I know that I feel concerned and that I care about other people, and yet the ones I talked to said that they experienced me as selfish, self-involved, and uncaring!" I have heard many such comments. So what do they have to do with acting? A lot, since you may think that you have created a complex emotional life on the stage only to find that a very small percentage of what you feel sees the light of day. What can you do about this kind if separation between impulse and expression? You can start by asking your friends and acquaintances for *scary* feedback, which is feedback that you might be frightened to hear. Make sure you tell people to level with you, since it is useless if they are just kind and polite.

Also, take Personal Inventory several times daily and challenge your own expression. In other words, ask yourself if you are expressing the sum total of what is going on inside. At first you may have to encourage or slightly exaggerate the impulses just to get them out. But after a short time, there will be fewer obstacles to your emotional impulses, and they will find their way out moment by moment.

Ask yourself if you have ever felt unseen or misperceived by others. If so, has it happened frequently? If it has, chances are that you're not giving the world enough to go on. Besides the obvious value to your acting that this emphasis on expressiveness offers, it will also enhance and improve the quality of your life.

You can get feedback anywhere at any time. You don't need special equipment, and it doesn't have to become a formal undertaking. In any kind of conversation you can ask another person for feedback without saying that you're doing an exercise.

INVOLVEMENT EXERCISES

The purpose of involvement exercises is to direct your concentration away from yourself toward an object or person outside yourself. By so doing, you eliminate tension, self-involvement, self-consciousness, and social-role obligations of many kinds.

Observe, Wonder, and Perceive
This exercise can be performed in several ways: silently or semiaudibly by yourself, or out loud with another person. Start simply by observing the things around you—people, inanimate objects, the weather, and so forth. Encourage yourself to wonder about the things that you observe. For example, look at a tree and observe its height, its colors, the shape of its leaves, the texture of the bark. Then you might wonder what kind of tree it is. How old? Does it grow in other parts of the country? Do animals live in it?

If you are observing a person, your flow of awareness might move like this:

I observe that he (or she) seems irritable. . .I wonder what's making him feel that way? . . . I perceive that he is really distracted and isn't listening to anybody . . . I wonder what he's thinking?. . .He keeps looking at his watch . . . I wonder why?. . . I wonder if he wants to be somewhere else? . . . He seems split between here and someplace other than here . . .

Very soon you will notice that you could go on indefinitely, perceiving, wondering, and becoming very involved with that person. You are no longer concerned with yourself, and the tension you started with is totally gone.

The two-people version of this exercise helps you relate to another actor and so stimulates a relationship as you prepare to work together in a scene. Observe, Wonder, and Perceive about the actor, which involves anything that you see, hear, smell, taste, or feel. You will observe things that are obviously there: "I observe that you feel a little rigid and are getting ready to do this exercise." You will perceive beyond what is obvious: "I perceive that you are trying to appear more relaxed than you really are." You perceive these things by noticing a subtle gesture, a fleeting expression, which might suggest protection or defensiveness: "I wonder if you are uncomfortable because of the exercise, or is it me?" Mostly you will wonder about things that you perceive sensorially. Your wonderings and perceptions can go into many areas, and if both actors do the exercise at the same time, the involvement with each other becomes total. As with any technique, your ability grows with practice and repetition. Your perceptions will deepen and your courage to wonder on a personal level will become part of it. I have seen some startling results with actors using this exercise, so try it and find out what happens for you.

Taking Responsibility for Others
In a group of people—a class or rehearsal group—express what you observe about each one of them as "selflessly" as possible, excluding the word "I" wherever you can. Try to help each person to be more effective by giving specific constructive suggestions. The word "responsibility" is the key to the exercise. If you really feel responsible for helping the other person, then something immediately becomes more important to you than yourself and your tension.

SELFLESS INVOLVEMENT

It is amazing how many people who act think that training is unnecessary. In fact, many of them hold the belief that training can actually interfere with the "natural, intuitive part of your talent." I'm not sure whether this is ignorance, superstition, or just plain rationalization for being lazy. Any kind of work takes some training, and a craft like acting, which deals with the physical, psychological, and emotional complexities of human behavior, takes the kind of training that lasts the better part of a lifetime. The stigma attached to studying—the notion that "If you are still in school, you must not be ready!"—is a mistake. Growth is a constant process and, with encouragement, will continue until the day you die.

The purpose of the Selfless Involvement exercise is to get you out of yourself, eliminate tension, involve yourself deeply in the life of another person, and get ready to act. Most actors have trouble with this exercise, and the main reason is their overwhelming involvement with themselves. Because of the nature of acting and the self-awareness it takes, you are constantly dealing with your instrument in one area or another. If you are not careful, after many years of this kind of self-involvement you can become cut off from the world around you.

Most of us know very little about the lives of others, including members of our own family. We usually relate on a very superficial social level to the people that we deal with. That kind of relationship becomes a habit, and years of the habit can cripple you and seriously affect your work. What can you do about it? The first step is to acknowledge that this problem might exist. Most people are convinced that they do care and that they are involved with the people around them. As you read these words, I'll bet you are thinking that you really know what is happening with the important people in your life. You probably feel that when it is time to become involved on the stage with other actors, you can do it easily. If you conduct some personal research, however, you may find it much more difficult than you imagined.

Select a friend whom you know pretty well and start by asking yourself:

How does that person feel most of the time?

What are that person's values? Principles?

What does he (she) want from life?

Where are his vulnerabilities?

What gives him joy?

What hurts him, and do I know when he is hurt?

What are his insecurities, and how does he deal with them?

How does he think?

What is he afraid of?

Whom does he love, and how does he love?

Is he honest in the expression of his feelings?

How much does he hide from view, and how do I know when he is hiding?

Is he happy? Unhappy?

How much of his behavior is ''cover'' behavior?

How does he really feel about me?

You could go on indefinitely asking these questions, and I'm certain you will be shocked to find how little you really know. What can you do from this point? Well, after you have acknowledged that there is work to be done, there are a number of good antidote exercises: Observe, Wonder, and Perceive is excellent, and so is Threshold of Interest. And most important, take Personal Inventory to discover when you are self-involved and how that manifests itself in your life—how it keeps you insulated from the world and the people in it.

Have lunch with a close friend and ask the questions detailed above. I'll bet that it will be the most satisfying lunch you ever had, and that you will get closer to your friend than ever before. Destructive habits are insidious and harmful to your growth, and self-involvement is one of the most intractable obstacles of all.

BUILDING A HEALTHY EGO

In the last lesson I wrote about keeping your ego out of your art. While it is very important to stay objective about criticism, you must also have the judgment to know the difference between an accurate and perceptive critique and a carping put-down. You can make the distinction if you have a solid craft and a functioning instrument. Do not misunderstand the need for ego; a healthy one is necessary to your work. In fact, actors who feel really good about themselves are rarely threatened by such questions as—

> Would I like to cover up or disguise some of my physical characteristics? How do I think other people see me? Am I concerned with how I sound? With how I move? Am I terrified at the thought of failing? Do I make excuses for myself? Do I feel that most of the other actors are better off than I am? Is the image I have of myself flattering? Am I embarrassed by my weaker emotions? Do I often feel as if I am on the outside looking in?

Almost everyone who is sensitive has felt some of these things. Unfortunately, if they go unattended they fester and multiply. They can modulate into the "oyster-pearl phenomenon," in which the actor compensates for them layer by layer, until the ego problems are covered by pearls of behavior that manifest themselves as competent, facile, "professional" acting.

When you identify an ego problem, admit its existence. Do not hide it or compensate for it. Ask yourself what can be done to change the way you feel. For example, if it is a physical problem, find out whether your feelings are rational or irrational. If you feel overweight, and in fact you are heavy, then what you must do to feel better about yourself is very clear. But you feel fat and you are not, the problem comes from another place. A poor ego state can affect everything you do and everything you feel.

There are many exercises and techniques you can use to build a healthy ego. Like physical exercise, you must keep at it over a long period of time. Get into a class that deals with the instrument; find a group that is involved in consciousness raising; get into therapy, if necessary. Help yourself in any way that you can.

EGO PREPARATIONS (PEP TALK)

Using your craft onstage or in front of the camera is totally dependent on your instrumental readiness. If you are truly ready to work, then you can; if you are not, all the craft in the world won't help. Everyone has acting problems and obstacles to functioning. What they are and how they manifest themselves is part of your daily work. Some common obstacles are tension, fear, the obligation to be a good actor, ego problems, dependencies, compensations, repetitious mannerisms, and so on, almost endlessly. All these problems and obstacles stand in the way of the actor, and they make it impossible to be impulsive, organic, and unpredictable. Unfortunately, far too many actors think that all you have to do is have talent and say your lines convincingly. Plenty of actors will say that the obstacles mentioned above are just a collection of complex words—that "You don't have to get so complicated in order to act; if you've got it, do it!"

In seventeen years of teaching actors, I have seen some enormously talented performers who were crippled by these problems. And I have seen equally gifted actors who never even came close to using their gifts because the obstacles made them incapable of touching that magic we refer to as talent.

"It's other actors that have to do it—not me. I'm different; it's all going to happen for me." I've seen the poor results of that kind of rationalization. You reap only what you sow; if you are really dedicated to the fullest development of your instrument, then you must commit yourself to a life of daily work. There are a lot of competitors, but very few champions. If you explore the elements that go into a champion or artist in any field, you discover that what they have in common besides talent is preparation and arduous work—daily involvement, without let-up, in what they do.

Another common trap is the notion that if you perform in a lot of scenes or plays, you will "get good" or grow. The truth is that without knowing or working in the proper areas, you will only solidify your bad habits. It's important that you work in scenes and plays, but while you are working, you must know how to use this valuable time. Among the daily exercises specifically designed to deal with obstacles are the relation group and Personal Inventory. While taking inventory, you may discover that you are frightened by the obligations of a particular piece of material. Or you may learn that, because you haven't worked in a while, you feel obligated to be good and impress people in an interview. Identifying an insecurity can lead you to do something to eliminate it so it won't stand in the way of being creative. In every instance where a problem exists, there is a technique that you can use to get rid of it.

EGO PREPARATIONS

When you work, it is always important to feel good about yourself.

Sense of Worth

The purpose of this exercise is to put you in touch with your genuine accomplishments. We often tend to forget or minimize things we have worked very hard to achieve. Go over the things that you have done in the past. Out loud to yourself, list your accomplishments and successes. Make sure that you emphasize your work and the nature of your involvement in it.

Count Your Blessings

Another good ego booster. List not only your accomplishments but everything in your life that is good: your health, your family, being loved, having good looks, being respected, and all the gifts life has bestowed on you.

Both exercises are helpful in raising your self-esteem, and I'll give you some more later. For now, practice them and remember this truth:

Desert your art for one day, and it will desert you for three!

MORE EGO PREPARATIONS

One of the most ego-nourishing activities is work. When you are working, you almost always feel worthy and good about yourself. Since employment in acting is inconsistent, even for actors who work often, they must keep themselves productive at all times. Your daily homework is vital to your craft and instrumental growth, and equally important to your ego state. You will be amazed at how good you feel about yourself after a week of working every day. The last lesson said that there are many ego preparations you can include in your schedule of work. This lesson describes more of them.

Remember to take Personal Inventory to find out where you are emotionally. Besides helping you reach a moment-to-moment BEING state, this exercise also identifies the problem area. You can't choose the right preparation if you don't understand the origin of the problem. For example, suppose that you are not happy with the way you look. By a process of elimination you can isolate exactly what you are unhappy about and set out to do something to correct it. If it is your hair style, you can change it. If it relates to being overweight, you can begin an exercise program. If it is more complex and requires some cosmetic adjustment, you can take care of that. A feeling of dissatisfaction with yourself can plague you for years, and since there is usually something you can do about it, identifying the problem is of the utmost importance.

The following list of ego preparations tells how you do them and what areas of ego difficulty they deal with.

Positivity
Selectively emphasize all the things around you that are positive. Relate only to the things that you feel good about. Starting with your environment, relate to the objects in the room that you like: a picture that brings back good memories, furniture that is comfortable, plants that you love, your pet, a piece of music that is uplifting, clothes you enjoy wearing, and so on. Go outside and respond to the beauty. Relate to the good odors, the animals, the sounds that make you feel good. Then do the same with yourself, relating only to your positive qualities. This exercise really changes a negative state to a positive one, and with practice it can help you eliminate ''down'' feelings.

LARGE COMMITMENTS

Yeah, Yeah!

Here is an old friend, the first exercise described in this book. Start by saying the word "Yeah!" and make it bigger each time until you are shouting. Get your body into it. Repeat the word and jump around until you feel elated.

Superman or Superwoman

You can do this the same general way you practice Yeah, Yeah! The difference is that you say: "I'm Superman/Superwoman; I'm faster than a speeding bullet! I can leap tall buildings in one bound . . . I can do *anything!*" At first you may feel a little silly, but I promise you that if you commit yourself to the exercise, you will be delighted by the results.

I Feel Terrific!

Again this is performed with a gigantic commitment, using your whole body. Start with a normal speaking tone and build with each expression until your voice and gestures are huge in size.

I have seen actors who were really depressed when they began these exercises, but who concluded by feeling elated, dynamic, and ready to work. Include the ego group in your daily work and watch your general ego state improve.

Jude doing a Superman exercise

INNER MONOLOGUE

If you have been working consistently on the exercises in this book, you are becoming more aware of your problems and obstacles. Try to get to the real BEING state at all times, especially before dealing with material. The various Personal Inventories will accomplish that. Once you feel "centered" and are expressing your moment-to-moment impulses without interference, then you can begin to approach the obligations of a given scene.

Being prepared to start working on choices for a scene doesn't mean that problems and obstacles won't present themselves as you work—they will!—but there are hundreds of tools you can use while working. Suppose that you have prepared properly and are really moving in the right direction, when all of a sudden you become tense and self-conscious and start to short-circuit the reality of your impulses. At this point most actors panic and begin to "behave": they start imposing life rather than dealing with the problem. Imposition of superficial behavior and assumption of nonorganic responses reach epidemic levels, and the acting goes down the tubes! Instead of panicking, however, you can acknowledge the problem, allow yourself to be aware of the tension, and *include* all this life in your behavior.

If you incorporate your discomfort and self-consciousness into the life of the scene, it will add dimension and color to your character rather than detract from it! You are probably thinking, "But won't the audience see that I'm tense and self-conscious? Won't it detract from the play?" The answer is no! Instead of presenting behavior that has no basis in reality, you are including your moment-to-moment reality. This doesn't interfere with anything that went on before or anything that follows, nor does it short-circuit your flow.

Another question I often hear is "Wait a minute; suppose the character isn't feeling tense or self-conscious at that point in the scene? Then what?" Here is my answer: "Isn't it possible that in the middle of a sentence, a person in a real-life situation can have other thoughts and feelings creep into the life that is taking place? Haven't you forgotten what you were going to say at times? Haven't you been affected by the presentation of a new stimulus and become tense or self-concerned? Of course you have; it's a common phenomenon. The reason we don't carry it onto the stage is that we create concepts of how the character would and would not behave—what he or she would and would not do in the scene. That is self-limiting! Every person you play is a human being just as you are, and anything that can happen to you in a life situation can happen to the character!"

A good way to hold yourself on the "reality track" is to keep an inner monologue going as you work. Carry on a Stream of Consciousness Monologue acknowledging the moment-to-moment feelings and thoughts that are occurring within you, and include the responses in the life of the scene.

For example, suppose you are doing a scene at a breakfast table with your wife. You read a newspaper. There is small talk between you. "How are you this morning, darling? Did you sleep well?" While this is going on, you may be feeling many things and having many thoughts, like "It's really hard to listen to her and read at the same time . . . I don't like this scene . . . I haven't anything to grab onto . . . What did she just say? . . . I don't know what to do with this scene . . . I wish she would slow down a little . . . I'm really uncomfortable," and so on.

This is the kind of life that might be going on in any scene, and if it exists, you should allow it to be included in your behavior. If you do not, and you try to function above it, all the reality that you're feeling is bottled up by your denial of those impulses, and you are left with superficial impositions. I know it will be difficult to try some of these techniques at first, especially if you have been working a different way for a long time. But if you have the courage to try, the rewards will amaze you. At first use them only in rehearsals; then when you achieve a little confidence with the approach, start to apply them to your professional work.

Remember that the three most important ingredients in artistic success are talent, discipline, and courage, and they are all dependent on each other.

TRUST

Actors have a great deal of difficulty making that first big commitment of expression—jumping in and going with what they feel. It is the same as the moment of terror just before an actor has to say his first line. All the doubts creep in, and all the little voices keep saying, "It's going to sound phony; I'm not ready! I don't believe it, I don't feel what I want to feel." All that commentary short-circuits you from BEING in the moment and expressing what you feel!

Of course, actors who function on a superficial level or those who are satisfied with presentational work do not fear unreality in their performance. But for sensitive actors who do fear it, and who suffer if they feel that they have fallen short of creating reality, *trust* is the antidote to that fear.

How do you gain trust? Well, it's not easy! Did you think I was going to say something stupid like "Just believe in yourself"? The world is full of advice-givers and old bromides, and usually they fail to help. Trust comes from a step-by-step process of finding out who you are and what you feel and learning that you have the right to BE and express who you are. It means taking your space in life and taking it on the stage. It comes from finding out *how* you feel in every living and acting situation and allowing those impulses to come out, no matter what you think the people around you expect. It comes from knowing the logic and meaning of a line of dialogue and *trusting* yourself to express that line in terms of what you really feel (even if it doesn't match your concept of the emotional obligation of the scene). It comes from encouraging yourself to flow with a moment-to-moment impulsivity, not redirecting what you feel into more acceptable social or theatrical behavior. It comes from taking the chances that sometimes make you look foolish. It comes from leaving yourself open to ridicule because you are BEING what you feel and the others around you are playing it close to the vest. It comes from having the courage to reach for your own authenticity.

Trust comes from doing all the work I write about in this book. It comes from your dedication and your daily work and the willingness to try . . . fail . . . try . . . fail . . . try some more . . . succeed . . . and start the process over again. Trust comes from avoiding the traps of complacency and false professionalism. The notion that if an actor studies his craft he is a student, not a "professional," is nonsense! Some of the people I teach have been studying with me for ten years or more. They work in films and television, and they come to class and work on their craft and their instrument. They grow month by month and year by year. There is no shortcut to trust. It comes from work . . . work . . . work!

COMMON ACTING PROBLEMS AND THEIR SYMPTOMS

Once in one of my directing seminar classes, a student director presented a scene with a talented actress who was filled with real emotion and a variety of interesting life that was never able to get free. Instead, she assumed emotional qualities that kept her on a level of sameness and predictability. I could see that a lot was going on within her that was being short-circuited by her inability to understand or deal with the problem. When I asked her what she was working for and *how* she was working for it, she could give only vague and general responses. Had she learned the how of it, she would have been functioning on a much higher level of creativity. In addition to knowing *how* to work, you must know what your specific obstacles are, *how* to identify them, and *how* to eliminate them. Here are the most common acting problems and their manifestations:

FUNCTIONING ABOVE TENSION

When you are tense and do not eliminate the tension, you try to function in spite of it. What happens is that all the real life remains locked up with the tension, and the audience gets the leavings: your expression of assumed emotional behavior.

IMPOSITION

To carry out his idea of what the material requires, an actor sometimes *imposes* that idea, adopting behavior that has little or nothing to do with what he is really feeling.

REDIRECTION

As a result of certain instrumental problems relating to the fear of exposure, embarrassment, and the like, actors may take what they are actually feeling at the moment and redirect it into a more comfortable emotional area. When your impulse is to cry, for example, you might redirect it into laughter because it is hard for you to expose that area of emotional life.

COMPENSATION

There are various kinds of compensational behavior. You've all seen actors who are obviously uncomfortable onstage and who assume a limp-wristed, relaxed pose. That is physical compensation. You've also noticed actors who try to communicate through their behavior that they are in better shape emotionally than they really are. That is emotional compensation.

DEPENDENCIES

Verbal, physical, intellectual, vocal, emotional, and other dependencies are created over a period of time as actors repeat things that they feel look good, sound good, and so on. You've often seen an actor enamored of his or her body, strutting around the stage in all kinds of physical postures that are not a result of what that person is really experiencing. Vocally dependent actors have developed an ability to arbitrarily indicate emotional life by manipulating their voices. Verbally facile actors love to roll words trippingly over their tongues in a romance with ornate language. All these dependencies cost the actor the excitement and unpredictability of organic reality.

PLAYING A QUALITY

The actor takes what often starts out to be a real impulse and indulges that emotion throughout a scene. Playing a quality involves milking an original truth into a predictable quality that doesn't change at all.

If you can see some of these problems in yourself, don't despair. Many of them are inter-related, and often you can overcome a whole group of obstacles with a single instrumental therapy approach. Just do your daily work!

MORE COMMON ACTING PROBLEMS

All actors have some obstacles that they must constantly work to overcome. Most of their problems are a result of never having learned a specific process of working, or of growing up in an inhibiting society. Naturally you cannot read a book and solve all your difficulties, so find a good class where you can become familiar with your particular problems. Doing a scene every week is important. A perceptive teacher can point out your obstacles and guide you in overcoming them.

Below are some more common acting problems.

SPLITS

Splits can be physical, intellectual, vocal, or emotional. Your instrument is divided into these four areas, and when you are functioning organically and naturally, the mind, the body, the voice, and the emotions operate as an integrated unit. At such times the body honestly expresses what you are feeling and thinking, and the voice is filled with the authenticity of the emotional life going on.

Splits occur when you attempt to express life that you don't feel, when you are self-conscious and cover up that discomfort, or when you are presenting an image which isn't consistent with your reality. Splits are easy to spot. Like a neon arrow, they point to the actor's problems.

You see an intellectual split when an actor is expressing a specific emotion but seems to be preoccupied or mentally located elsewhere.

A physical split is obvious when the body has little or no relationship to the quality of the emotion being expressed. Everyone has watched actors screaming onstage while their bodies fall into some limp pose or freeze rigid with tension. They may occasionally lift an arm in the midst of their tirade and abruptly drop it to their side. It looks unnatural, and that's because it is.

A vocal split occurs when the actor verbally expresses an emotion that has nothing to do with what he feels. Vocal splits are common in vocally dependent actors.

Emotional splits follow the same pattern: the actor either experiences one kind of emotional life and expresses another, or completely suppresses everything he feels and imposes life over that reality. The instrument cannot lie!

LOGIC

Understanding the material and the logic of every scene is important so that you can organically fulfill the material. However, another trap for actors is to impose behavior that is logical. They behave the way the character is supposed to, without creating any of the realities that would make the person really feel that way. It's called "playing logic."

ASSUMPTIONS

Sometimes an actor *assumes* the probable responses to what is going on in a scene rather than allowing his organic response to develop. When people in a scene are in the midst of a heated argument, for example, one of the actors might say to himself, "My character wouldn't respond that way." He immediately assumes behavior that he feels is proper for the character instead of allowing himself to respond in the way he is really being affected. Thus he short-circuits his own reality and is left with assumed life that has no real basis.

Most of these problems are interrelated in one way or another. Don't become one of the actors who suffer from "theatrical immortality"—the fraudulent belief that "I don't have those problems . . . I don't need to get involved in the classroom . . . it may be right for others, but I'll make it without all that analytical crap." The problems that you have will follow you to your grave if you don't eliminate them! The coming lessons deal with the antidotes.

ANTIDOTES FOR COMMON ACTING PROBLEMS

Acting should and can be fun. Once you have eliminated your obstacles, it is possible that you will experience an enjoyment you never knew before. To recapitulate, here are the problem areas listed in the last two lessons: functioning above tension, imposition, redirection, compensation, dependencies, playing a quality, splits, logic, assumptions.

The first principle is that if you arrive at a BEING state and can maintain it, every one of these problems will vanish. In my opinion, the concept of BEING is the bridge between process and the application of that process. When you are comfortable with everything that you feel and when you are expressing what you feel from moment to moment, you need not do any more or less than what you feel. You experience no tension, so *you do not have to function above it.* If you are organically expressing all that is real, you will not be tempted to impose anything. Since the basis for any BEING state is comfort with what you feel, there won't be any occasion to redirect your emotions into more comfortable areas. Compensation, like the other problems, comes from trying to communicate something other than what is actually going on. Since you are all of a piece, impressively and expressively, when you are in the BEING state, there is no need to compensate.

Because the state of BEING is the major antidote to the common problems of acting, the exercises which help you to arrive at and maintain that state are the ones to practice. Following are suggestions for using them to work on specific problems.

TENSION

Instead giving way to panic when you become aware of that demon, tension, creeping up your spine, acknowledge its existence. Allow your tension to express itself as part of the life that is happening in the scene. After you have included the tension in the scene, involve yourself with your choice and with your acting partner. Involvement is the enemy of tension.

IMPOSITION

When you become aware of the difference between what you really feel and what you are imposing in a scene, include this awareness and encourage the underlying reality to express itself. If you feel that something is wrong but don't know exactly what, take a Personal Inventory. Ask yourself, "How do I feel? . . . Am I expressing that? . . . If not, why not? . . . What can I do about it?" By taking a Personal Inventory you automatically stop the imposed behavior and direct your energies to the real impulses. Commit yourself to working for whatever choice will stimulate the life you are supposed to experience in the scene. Then you will be using your time productively, and you will not return to imposing.

REDIRECTION

Redirection usually occurs when a particular emotion is uncomfortable or embarrassing. Here again, include your discomfort in the life of the scene; then incorporate the real impulses that are under the discomfort. Of course, redirection comes from living habits and patterns that may span your entire adult life. You must work to eliminate the causes of your discomfort with any emotional state. All the BEING exercises encourage the acceptance of everything you feel.

COMPENSATION

Handle these in the same way as redirection problems.

DEPENDENCIES

Many dependencies have been acquired over years of acting and training and have become solidified with repetition. The best way to start eliminating them is to know that they exist. If you encourage the expression of reality, most of them will evaporate. You cannot sustain a vocal dependency, for example, when you are committed to the real underlying emotion. If they are allowed to emerge, those natural feelings can be expressed in all their color through the voice.

MANNERISMS AND BEHAVIORAL DEPENDENCIES

What are mannerisms—"schticks"—"numbers"? We hear actors, directors, and teachers talk about them a lot. What they are to me are external behavioral expressions which actors develop that have little or no connection with their inner reality. Because something works for a particular actor at one time or another, he consciously or unconsciously adopts the mannerism as part of his "personality." Multiply these mannerisms by fifty and you have an actor who is nothing more than a bag of tricks. You have seen actors who do exactly the same things from film to film. You know how they will respond long before they do, because you've seen it happen so many times before. It is not enough for an actor to recognize these dependencies; he must understand their origin and the reason he acquired them to begin with.

The most common reason for developing mannerisms is that an actor has certain fears or phobias. We grow up with a number of emotional taboos, and they become older and stronger as we do. Some emotions are difficult to feel or express, and we learn to shy away from them. After a time we are not even aware that we don't have that emotional color in our rainbow. An actor who is given a role containing many of these taboo emotions has to "fake" it, even if he cons himself into thinking otherwise.

Another common cause of mannerisms is a lack of organic connection. An actor who learns to perform externally develops many ways of behaving that have nothing to do with reality, since he doesn't start from a basis of reality. These mannerisms become dependable tricks for representing the emotion of the character. Since they are impositional (just laid on top), they have no real emotional foundation. They are always the same.

What can be done to eliminate these insidious mannerisms that we all acquire over the years? Have the courage to admit their existence, and then trace their origin as best you can. If they come from conditioned fears, embark on an emotional therapy (acting therapy) project to eliminate those fears. There are a great number of exercises designed just for that purpose. If your dependencies are a result of working too "technically" or externally, start thinking about how to work more organically. Get into a good class and reeducate your instrument.

These antidotes may seem complex and long-drawn-out, but they are not really. Once you start doing the work, you will be amazed at how quickly your instrument responds. The truth is the most natural thing for us to deal with!

OBSTACLES TO YOUR EMOTIONAL FREEDOM

Suppose that a person grows up with a number of taboos and fears and as a result becomes insulated and self-protective. He finds it almost impossible to show or express need, warmth, softness, love, or deep affection, for fear that he might become vulnerable. Over many years his irrational fears grow into solid blocks. Now, imagine compounding these fears with other areas of irrational belief, and the person who emerges has many obstacles to feeling and expressing.

If this person decides to become an actor, he comes to the stage with a multitude of inhibitions, some of which he is not even conscious of. In every role he approaches, there are emotional obligations calling for responses that he is unable to kindle. What can he do to change? First, he must be willing to admit the existence of the obstacles; second, he must start on the road to eliminate them—the road of instrumental therapy.

I believe that if you confront your demons consistently, you will ultimately defeat them! I ask my students to do the most difficult things first, for when they accomplish those, everything less intimidating becomes nonexistent. If you are terrified to show need and you do an exercise that obligates you to express extreme need, you tear down not only the obstacles that keep you from expressing need, but the many doors behind that wall. You discover that you have access to softness, affection, tenderness—the spectrum of all your needs. With repeated onslaughts the walls vanish, and you can allow yourself to feel all the emotions that you have spent a lifetime denying. Now when you set foot on the stage, you are no longer dependent on the presentation of emotions, but are fully affected and expressive of what you feel.

Whether or not you will deal with your obstacles isn't a matter of choice; if you want to be an artist, you *must* eliminate them. Ask yourself some important questions:

> Am I happy with my work?
> Are there areas of emotion I avoid?
> How much fear do I experience when I act?
> Do I premeditate responses?
> Am I comfortable socially? Theatrically?
> Do I totally express everything I feel?
> How often do I get embarrassed?
> Do certain roles or emotional areas make me anxious?

Your answers will help you identify the obstacles to your emotional freedom.

DAILY WORK SCHEDULE

The payoff for your acting exercises comes when your daily work begins to bear fruit. As a young actor, I came to craft training at a time when I was dissatisfied with my work and helpless to do anything about it. I took to the training as a thirsty man takes to water. I became so enthralled with Sense Memory that I worked as many as five hours a day in this area alone. I would sometimes be involved in rehearsing five scenes at one time. My entire day was taken up with craft, and I loved it! Naturally I had difficulties, but I regarded them as humps to climb over. For a long time my greatest satisfactions came from involvement with my work. I spent every Monday, Wednesday, and Friday morning for a year at the zoo, where I studied animal behavior and mannerisms and even designed my own techniques for achieving the sense of an animal. Every week I did a scene in class; some weeks I did two. I continued to go on interviews for acting jobs in films and television.

Suddenly one day in class in the midst of a scene, it all came together. The choices I worked for stimulated the life I was after, one emotional impulse gave way to another. I felt impulsive and unpredictable—and good, as if I were flying. After that the experience of total functioning came more and more frequently, and soon I was able to "push my buttons" in readings. I could identify the obligation, know what they wanted, and in a short time, stimulate that reality for myself.

The sensation of being a craftsman made me feel special and terrific. I walked around with a smile on my face, as if I had some fantastic secret. I saw other actors tense and struggling, and instead of feeling better than they were, I wanted to share my wonderful secret with them. As I look back on that period, I see that they were some of the best years of my life.

The most important point that I can share with you about these experiences is that they would never have happened without the daily commitment. Make this commitment with yourself to do the following exercises.

Sensory Inventory
In addition to Sense Memory practice, where you work with and without an object, try to find out how your senses function. What are the peculiarities of your apparatus? Which senses are stronger than others, and specifically, how do they work? Challenge them . . . have fun with them.

Observe, Wonder, and Perceive
Don't forget this one. You can do it alone or with another person. Simply ask yourself questions about things and people as you become curious about them. Pick up on behavior, and look for things that you have not been aware of before.

Impulsivity Work

Impulsivity exercises are helpful in getting you to trust your moment-to-moment life. Practice impulsivity every day, particularly if you have problems in this area. A really good one is Essence Impulsivity. Look around a room in your house and express in sound and movement your impulsive response to each object in the room. Do it very fast, so that you go from one object to another carrying each response into the next.

DAILY WORK SCHEDULE CONTINUED

It can be very difficult to work alone for hours on end without receiving any feedback or appreciation. Pretty soon you begin to wonder why you are doing it. Daily work is like building a bank account: saving a few dollars every week doesn't seem like much, but at the end of a couple of years you have a chunk of money. Once you have established a routine for practicing your craft, it becomes easier. Find the right times and the right places to work. Choose exercises that you enjoy and can look forward to doing. Occasionally involve a friend in them. Do a lot of work outside your house, in places like the Farmers' Market, the zoo, restaurants, and the like.

Start the day by taking Personal Inventory to find out what you are feeling and what obstacles are preventing the expression of those feelings. If you are constipated with anger and are functioning above it, do a Dump exercise. Or if you try it and find that it doesn't release the internal demons, go on to an Abandonment exercise. You can explore the Primal Moan described in this lesson, or a series of large sounds. There are plenty of exercises in the expurgative area.

If your problems do not require Expurgative exercises, diagnose them and find the right antidote. Imagine that you awaken one morning and seem to feel fine—at peace with yourself and the world. You begin to do a Personal Inventory, only to realize that your peace stems from apathy. You feel all right, but not excited, stimulated, affectable, or responsive toward anything. Although this is a common state that we all experience from time to time, it's deceptive. You think everything is fine when in fact you are simply insulated. You are protecting yourself from feeling anything because it is less upsetting or painful to establish that state. Indeed, this insulated condition often eludes the scrutiny of Personal Inventory. One thing to look for while doing the Inventory is a *variety* of impulses. If they all seem to be on the same level, dig deeper! A good strategy when you are insulated in this way is to work on the vulnerability exercises:

Primal Moan

This can double as an expurgative as well as a vulnerability exercise. Start in the fetal position on the floor and encourage a deep, gut-level moan. Continue to moan, holding the sound of each one for a long time, and begin a rocking motion. Soon you should sense the locked-up impulses floating to the surface. You can expect to start crying or feeling extremely vulnerable. If this exercise does not work as well for you as it should, try others in the vulnerability group.

Dying

Pretend that you have only five minutes to live. You are lying in bed talking with everyone who is important to you. Surround yourself with all the people in your life with whom you have unfinished business, and tell them anything you wish. You have nothing to lose! Most people break down and establish a real emotional flow in this vulnerability exercise.

Surround Yourself with Meaningful Objects

In your sensory imagination, create around you the meaningful objects, people, and places in your life, past and present. Talk to them and talk to yourself about them. In your fantasy put something that you can relate to in every part of the room.

Keep in mind that instrumental work is like practicing to be a juggler; if you exercise every day, your entire body becomes attuned to juggling. Form the habit of daily work and you will begin to look forward to it!

A BALANCED WORK PROGRAM (SENSE MEMORY)

Create a balanced work program for yourself. Be sure to give it variety; if you do the same thing over and over each day, it becomes tedious. And make it a point to divide your time equally between instrument and craft. The basic exercises in preparation, relaxation, sensitizing, and Personal Inventory are important starters, but you don't need to do the same ones all the time. Try a mixture of relaxation exercises: Rag Doll, Logy, Tense and Relax, Weight and Gravity, and so on. You can try many ways to sensitize, and Personal Inventory is always changing.

Sense Memory is a daily involvement; do at least a half-hour of it during your workday. The purpose is to train yourself to create objects on the stage when they don't really exist. Work with something to eat or drink, since it involves all five senses. Start with the most logical sense. For example, unless you close your eyes and try to create an object tactilely, you should begin with the visual sense.

Sense Memory is trained by asking questions about the object that are "answered" *only* by the sense that you relate the question to. How tall is the object? (Let your eyes see its height.) What is its shape? (Your eyes will determine the shape; do not answer the question intellectually.) What are its colors? How many colors are there? How do they blend with each other? How does the light affect the object? Where are the shadows? You may ask twenty or thirty visual questions, or you may ask only ten and move on into the tactile area. Periodically put the object aside and work without it, asking the same questions that you did when it was in front of you. Then go back to the real object and see how close your sensory responses were. In the Sense Memory exercise it is very important to involve all your senses, since they interrelate and strengthen your feeling of reality. The kinds of questions you ask come from the object itself.

Have fun with your Sense Memory exercises; don't fall into the trap of being too clinical. Ask questions that appeal to you, and you will soon develop the ability to explore the objects adventurously. In addition to your full-scale Sense Memory workouts, play around with simple choices—meaningful objects that stimulate an emotional response, like a photograph of an old girlfriend. Work with and without these objects until you can re-create them enough to be affected by them. Try many simple choices each day to enrich your Sense Memory workout. One of their chief values is that they yield immediate emotional results and will keep you practicing Sense Memory. After a couple of months, start to identify the obligations in a scene and find simple choices that you can approach sensorially, to stimulate the desired emotional life.

A BALANCED WORK PROGRAM (ELIMINATING OBSTACLES)

After a period of daily workouts you will hit your stride, starting with instrumental preparation and moving to Sense Memory work. Set aside some time to deal with material; monologues are fine if you have difficulty getting other people to work with you regularly. Choose a piece of material where the obligations are clear and simple. Identify a single emotional obligation, and ask yourself what you can work for that might stimulate the emotion for you. Whenever possible, approach the choice through the sensory process. Using Sense Memory to create objects is a way to affect yourself emotionally. Using the sensory process repeatedly helps you to make it yours. A well-balanced daily work schedule should allow for exploration of material about three times a week.

Devote a large part of your time to identifying obstacles and working to eliminate them. For example, suppose you have difficulty with conflict. That is to say, you are "conflict phobic," and you have avoided conflict of any kind for most of your life. In such a case you would choose to do exercises that deal specifically in conflict areas: Dump, Exorcism, Imaginary Monologues aimed at people you have conflict with, Abandonment, Anger and Rage workouts, and so on.

On the other hand, you may have difficulty with the lighter emotions like humor and laughter. It may be hard for you to have fun. If that is the case, there are a whole bunch of fun exercises: Silly Dilly, Yeah! Yeah! selectively emphasizing all the funny things in a room, the Must Game, and many more.

If you are male and have been told all your life that sissies cry and men don't, you probably have a well-developed resistance to vulnerability. In that case, identify all the things in the world which make you vulnerable, and concentrate on creating them. Imagine that people you love are hurt or ill. Reminisce about meaningful times in your life. Conduct imaginary monologues with important people, talking about things that will elevate your vulnerability.

Whatever your problems are, there are exercises that will eliminate them. Understand, however, that it has taken you many years to establish these obstacles and that they will stubbornly resist leaving. You must work in an area for a period of time before you can expect total elimination of that problem. Since we all have a number of areas that inhibit us, don't try to take on too many at once. You know what areas you have the most difficulty in, and those are the ones to tackle first.

Dont't assume that the daily work schedule is an arduous and tedious involvement that deals only with the weight of your problems. It can be a lot of fun and very fulfilling, too. Remember: Every day that you work, you invest in your instrumental and craft bank account.

NOTES

NOTES

NOTES

THE CRAFT

THE CRAFT

In this section on craft, the lessons present exercises and techniques that help you to create realities on the stage or in front of a camera. The playwright gives you a set of circumstances to deal with and obligations to fulfill. You, the actor, must have a process that you can use to affect yourself the way the character in the material is affected. That process is called craft.

Before the actor can approach the craft, his or her instrument must be prepared to function. Preparation is largely a matter of clearing the blocks and obstacles that keep you from being emotionally affected and freely expressing your impulses. When you have accomplished this BEING state, you are ready for the elements of craft: the *choices* and the *approaches* that lead you to fulfillment of the material.

Actors too often lose sight of the purpose of all the exercises and workshop training. You prepare your instrument so that you can *act*—so that you can bring to the stage or the film all those living impulses the author wrote about.

Craft is a toolbox filled with a variety of implements that you select to use at the right time and in the right place. Learn how to use these tools expertly and you will be able to do what *you* decide to, rather than being at the mercy of chance. The word "craftsman" designates one who knows exactly what he or she is doing and how to do it.

WHAT IS SENSE MEMORY?

Have you worked with Sense Memory? Do you know what it is? When I ask actors those questions, invariably they respond, "Sure. Oh, yeah . . . for years." Yet it usually turns out that they not only don't know how to do a Sense Memory exercise, but have no idea why it is used or what it is supposed to accomplish. Sense Memory has the distinction of being the most misunderstood process in the Method. From Stanislavski to the present time, it has been mistaught, misinterpreted, fragmented, and misused to the point of ambiguity.

Sense Memory it is simply the sensory memory—the five senses memorizing the response you have had to real objects. As explained in the previous section, it is the technique that gives you the ability, first with the real object and later without it, to re-create an object when it is not really there.

Why do you do that? Is it just an actor's homework? Do you do it to sharpen the senses so that you can respond to the things around you more sensitively? Yes! You do it for that purpose—and more.

Sense Memory is used to create an object (a place, a person, an inanimate object, an animal, a piece of music, a temperature, and the like) when the object does not really exist. The whole purpose is to stimulate the response that you would have to that object if it were present. If the object once had an emotional impact on you, and you want to feel that way in a scene, you can re-create the object in order to stimulate the emotional life required by the scene. You are working not for a simple response, but for a complete relationship filled with many colors and a variety of impulses. The purpose of Sense Memory, then, is to be able to re-create any object or group of objects in order to stimulate a complex inner organic life that fulfills the intention of the scene or play.

In order to use this magnificent tool, you must spend many hours over a period of years perfecting your skill with Sense Memory. When you truly master the process, it can take you anywhere you want to go! You must spend many hours practicing it, but the rewards are enormous!

The next time you hear someone talk about Sense Memory, ask what it is, how it is used, and for what purpose.

Anna doing a Sense Memory exercise with a cup of coffee

SENSE MEMORY

We are the sum total of all that has entered our consciousness through the five sensory doors, so it is only logical to return to the senses when we wish to stimulate emotions. Far too many actors and teachers separate the sensory process from acting itself. They make it a classroom practice involvement instead of a magnificent tool to be used onstage or in front of the camera. Sense Memory is an integral part of other choice-approach areas, and as such becomes a foundation to much of the work of acting.

In a given scene, you as the actor have many emotional obligations set down by the author. In order to feel the way the script tells you that the character feels, you must do something to make yourself experience the same life as the character. Knowing that a certain object affects you in a certain way, you decide to "work" for that object in hopes that it will stimulate the desired life. The way you work for the object can be through the use of Sense Memory. If you are successful in creating the object sensorially, you can expect to be affected by it.

Long before you use Sense Memory on the stage, however, you must spend many hours practicing it—for like a pianist, the actor must practice every day. Practice consists of doing Sense Memory exercises so that your senses will respond with growing accessibility.

If you have been taking sensory inventories, you have already started to be more familiar with each sense, its peculiarities, and its responses to objects. Put aside some time each day to do Sense Memory. Find a place with few distractions and select a period when you don't have other obligations. Early in the morning or late at night are good times to work.

The Sense Memory Exercise

When you start to do Sense Memory, it's best to choose an object that utilizes all five senses, like something to eat or drink. If you drink coffee, that is a good object to practice on. With the cup on the table in front of you, start asking sensory questions. You can begin with any of the senses, but I have found that starting with the *visual* sense allows you to place the object spatially and helps when you are working without it. Respond to the questions sensorially; do *not* answer them intellectually or verbally.

For example: "What is the shape of the object?" Let your eyes answer with what they see. "How high does the object stand from the tabletop?" Again, the response is what you see. And the same with other questions: "How wide is the object? . . . From the angle that I see it, how far into the object can I see? . . . Where in the object is the liquid? . . . How do the colors blend into each other? . . . What does the texture look like? . . . How many different textures are there? . . . How does the light affect the object? . . . Are there any reflections? . . . Are there any shadows? . . . How long is the shadow . . . What is its shape?"

After you have asked twenty or thirty questions, you might put the object aside and work without it, asking the same questions you did when it was in front of you. When you are working to re-create it, put the object out of visual range so that your eyes do not become confused. Ask the questions and let the visual sense try to see the object as it was when it was there. After you have gone through the process, but the cup back exactly where it was and take a quick inventory to see what you were successful in re-creating and what you did not deal with.

At this point, introduce the *tactile* sense and ask questions in that area; "As I touch the object with two fingers, what do I feel? . . . Where exactly are the points of contact? . . . What does the texture feel like? . . . What is the temperature? . . . With which finger do I feel the most?" Remember, the responses to these questions are taking place in the exact spot of each finger that is making contact with the cup! Touch the cup with your other fingers. With each one ask, "What does it feel like as the finger makes contact? . . . How much more or less do I feel with this finger than with the others? . . . How does the temperature differ from my own body temperature? . . . How long does it take to equalize?"

With all five fingers on the cup, you might lean forward and involve your *olfactory* sense. "How close do I come to the cup before I smell anything? . . . What is the first odor? . . . Where in my nose does the smell really take place?" Remember that the answers to all these questions come only from your olfactory sense; do not answer them intellectually. "How many different odors do I smell?" As you lean over the cup, you probably experience the steam or heat of the liquid on your face. Deal with it! "Where do I feel the heat?" . . . What does it feel like? . . . Can I see the steam? . . . What shapes does it take?"

Note that while you were working with the olfactory sense, you had to involve the tactile (the heat rising from the cup) and the visual (the steam you saw) because they are sensory realities. You must acknowledge their existence or you will violate the object's reality. If you ignore the other sensory realities while working without the object, it is almost impossible for the senses to re-create the object. As you lean toward the cup, you might see more of the liquid. Explore the colors, the way the cream in the coffee takes shapes as it blends, and possibly your own reflection. At any point after a group of questions, put the object aside and work without it. After asking the same questions, always return to it. When you work with Sense Memory for a while you will discover what kinds of questions appeal to your senses—which ones elicit the greatest response. Be adventurous!

At this point, start to *lift* the object. Be careful not to take anything for granted. In this simple act of lifting the cup to your lips—a movement that you make many times a day—there are perhaps a hundred sensory questions you might ask. With all five fingers touching the object, ask yourself: "How much pressure must I exert to grasp the object firmly? . . . Where does that pressure start? . . . What muscles are involved? . . . What happens? . . . As my fingers tighten into the object, what happens? . . . How much resistance does each finger encounter? . . . How far into each finger's pad does the object penetrate?'' Respond with each finger individually, since the angle and the pressure vary with each one. "How and where do I feel the muscular tension in my hand? . . . How and where do I feel it in my wrist? . . . How far up the arm can I feel the muscles tighten? . . . Does the heat of the object increase with the pressure? . . . If so, where do I feel the variations in temperature? . . . What tells me that I am applying the proper pressure to start lifting the object?''

You could ask twenty or thirty questions without even being close to lifting the cup, because an incredible number of things happen physically in this action. "As I prepare to slowly lift the object off the table, what is the very first thing that takes place? . . . Where does the movement start in my hand, arm, wrist, shoulder? . . . What happens to each finger? . . . How does the pressure change? . . . As the object barely begins to leave the surface of the table, what do I feel in my hand, fingers, etc.? . . . When do I first feel weight? . . . What is weight? . . . How does this feeling of weight affect each finger? . . . What does the downward pull of the object feel like in each finger? . . . How does it feel in my wrist? . . . How far up the arm do I feel the weight of the object?'' As you lift the object to your face, the angles changed, and with that change different muscles are involved. You must deal with all the variations of pressure and all the new muscles that come into play.

Ask questions about the muscles you involve as you change the angle of your arm. As you lift the cup to your lips and tilt your head slightly backward, ask questions about what you see as your head tilts back. Then ask about the object again. "As I lift the cup closer to my lips, when do I feel the heat? . . . At what point and where on my face do I feel it? . . . How does the temperature differ from my body temperature?'' And so on. Again, the questions are answered not in the mind, but with the sense itself. When the cup is close to your mouth, be sure to deal with all the senses that come into play. What you see, what you feel, what you smell. "How far does my head go back as I prepare to receive the liquid? . . . As the cup makes contact with the lower lip, what is my first sensation?. . . What is the texture of the object on my lip? . . . What is the temperature? . . . How long does it take for my lip to acclimate to the heat? . . . What do I feel in my arm? . . . What do I feel in my hand? . . . As I bring the object closer to my mouth, at what point do I involve the top lip? . . . What does it feel like? . . . When my top lip makes contact with the object, what does that feel like? . . . How does it differ from the bottom lip? . . . How much further back must I tilt my head to get the liquid? . . . What happens to my arm and hand? . . . What new pressures do I feel as I do this?''

While you're practicing, it is very important that you BE—that you include everything you feel in your work, all your thoughts and impulses, and allow yourself to express them freely. If it's tedium you're experiencing, put that feeling into the questions you ask. Life goes on no matter what you are doing, whether you are working on a scene, performing in a film, or practicing a Sense Memory exercise.

"With the cup at my lips, can I feel the liquid sloshing around? . . . Do I see it? . . . What does it look like from this angle? . . . What sounds does it make? . . . What are the sounds in the room? . . . Can I smell the coffee? . . . What does it smell like? . . . How many different odors do I detect? . . . Can I smell cream? . . . Sugar? . . . The coffee itself? . . . With which nostril do I smell the most?" You might experiment by blocking one nostril at a time to see where and how you are smelling the object.

At any point you may want to stop and work with the object in small areas. For instance, when the cup is closest to your face, you're seeing, smelling, feeling, and hearing all at once. Your senses are being flooded with stimulation. So you might have to break it down and take it in small hunks, working separately with each sense and then putting them together.

As the liquid goes into my mouth, what part of my mouth does it hit first? . . . At the exact moment of contact with the liquid, what do I feel? . . . What is the temperature? . . . What is the sensation of temperature? . . . What is the difference in temperature between the inside of my mouth and the liquid? . . . What in my mouth tells me that? . . . What is the path of the liquid as it runs into my mouth? . . . What parts of the mouth does it touch? . . . What are the many sensations I am experiencing in my mouth? . . . Can I smell the liquid internally? . . . As it runs back into my mouth, are there any sensitive teeth? . . . Do I feel any pain in any parts of the gums and inner cheeks? . . . How long does it take for the liquid to equalize to my mouth's temperature? . . . What is the consistency of the liquid? . . . What does it feel like on my tongue? . . . What are the *taste* sensations? . . . Where do I begin to taste? . . . What is taste? . . . Where in my mouth am I actually tasting what I taste? . . . How many different tastes can I identify? . . . Can I distinguish the separate ingredients of the liquid? . . . What happens when I begin to swallow? . . . What are the various muscular activities I feel? . . . What does my tongue do? . . . What does my head do?" Take the exercise to the conclusion of replacing the cup on the table. Work with this object for as long as it takes to really explore it totally.

The simple action of relating to the cup of coffee on the table, lifting it to your mouth, taking a sip, and setting the cup down is the entire Sense Memory exercise. You must specifically explore all the sensory elements that are involved in order to be able to re-create the action without the object. Working with this simple object could take several weeks. Do not lose sight of the reasons for practicing Sense Memory. You are concentrating on the cup of coffee in order to train your senses to re-create any object in imaginary terms. You need this training so that you can work for meaningful objects on the stage. Successfully re-creating meaningful objects will ultimately stimulate the emotional life you need in order to fulfill the obligations of the material.

As you practice your Sense Memory exercises you will become aware that your senses are growing more responsive to everything. You will begin to notice things around you that you were never conscious of; you will feel temperature changes more acutely; you will taste your food with increased appreciation; and people will take on added behavioral dimensions. These are some of the rewards of elevating your sensory accessibility.

The beauty of Sense Memory is that you can practice it anywhere. It takes no special equipment, and you can even carry your sensory objects in your pocket. You can make music in dead silence; you can create beautiful things even when you are surrounded by ugliness. The world is at the command of your imagination through the magic of your five doors of perception.

Two of the most important purposes of Sense Memory are your instrumental development—the training of your senses to be alive and responsive—and the development of your ability to create the realities you need in order to make you feel what the character in a script feels. If you really commit yourself to Sense Memory, practice it daily, and make it a part of your life, it will become a tool which elicits unconscious organic responses of astounding dimension.

Ask as many questions as you need in order to re-create the object you are working for. As you go along, you'll find your own rhythm and your own sensory needs. In the beginning your instrument may require more questions than it will later on. You may have to ask more questions in certain sensory areas than in others, since some senses are naturally weaker than others. You may have to isolate one question and ask thirty questions related to it before your senses respond to that specific area of the object.

The nature of the object will often dictate its own investigative process. Choosing objects is a very important consideration. Remember that an object can be anything: a sound, a smell, the temperature, a person, an animal, and many other things. As I said earlier, at first you should choose objects to eat or drink, since they involve all five senses. As you progress, you'll find many reasons behind your choice of an object. To develop a sense like the tactile area, which is relatively sluggish in most people, you might work with a variety of textures and materials. If you have a weak auditory sense, practice with music or objects that produce sounds. Choose objects that excite you and interest you emotionally or sensorially, so you won't get bored.

Sensory Checklist
The following questions provide a checklist to help with your sensory work. Don't use it like a pilot's checklist, literally checking off each item as you do the exercise. Rather, refer to it from time to time as a guide. Look it over before you begin to work and then put it aside. Soon the checklist will be internalized and become part of your work.

Am I asking enough questions?
Am I asking the questions specifically?
Do my senses understand the questions?
Am I asking the right kinds of questions?
Do my questions interest me?
Do they affect me emotionally?
How do I feel moment by moment? Am I including that in the process?
Am I asking inventive and imaginative questions?

Are my questions coming in logical sequence, or are they violating the
chronological order?
Am I using my time well?
Do I have any tension?
Am I doing it for me?
Am I getting a sense of the object? Do I really feel it, taste it, smell it, see it?
Am I tricking myself, surprising my senses?
Do I encourage the object to suggest its own exploration?
Am I including everything that is going on?
How can I have more fun with this object?
Am I letting the exercise stimulate thoughts and feelings?
Am I really working sensorially, or just suggestively?
Have I located the object in space?
Am I asking supportive questions in each category?
Am I using the stronger senses to encourage the weaker ones?
Am I being adventurous?

As you use the checklist, add your own items to it. Have fun and enjoy the
process—all the while knowing that if you master Sense Memory as an acting tool,
you will stand far above the actors who say their jokes, take their money, and run.

VARIATIONS ON SENSE MEMORY

In Sense Memory work the entire world is at your fingertips. At home you can continue prac-
ticing with your cup of coffee, and when you are out on interviews or just out having lunch,
you can carry a variety of small objects in your pocket. The value of doing Sense Memory
wherever you go is that it becomes a part of your life and it isn't restricted to homework.

As soon as you feel that you are beginning to have some success with the exercise, carry it into
your scene work. Start with very simple choices. Let me define choice and obligation:

The *obligation* in a scene is that emotional life you desire to feel as dictated by the
material.

The *choice* is that which you work for in order to fulfill the obligation.

For example, in a particular scene you might decide that the emotional *obligation* is to feel irritated. So you might *choose* to work for a nagging headache because when you have one everything seems to irritate you. Or you might identify the *obligation* as a feeling of love and affection. Then you might *choose* to re-create sensorially a photograph of someone you love. The more you practice Sense Memory as clinical exercise work, the more quickly you will be able to incorporate it into your acting.

Besides the conventional Sense Memory exercises, there are literally hundreds of sensory techniques you can use to heighten your facility.

You might recall the voice of a person you used to know but don't see anymore. Try to re-create every quality of that voice. Of course, you can do the same exercise with any object.

Sense Memory Workout
Explore any inanimate object—
   then work without it.
Get familiar with an animate object like a person or animal—
   then work without it.
Explore a part of your own body—
   then work without it.
Explore an object that comes in contact with your body, like a hat, dress, or shirt—
   then work without it.
Investigate a sound or smell—
   then work without it.
Isolate a group of objects that you can taste—
   then work without it.

Attempt to sensorially re-create all these objects hours later. This process trains the senses to reach for previous sensory stimulation.

On-the-Spot Sense Memorizing
Every day you experience many things. Pick a fleeting experience: a bus passes you, and the fumes hit your face . . . A telephone rings in another room . . . You take the first sip of a cold beer on a hot day at the beach. Just after it is gone, try to re-create the sensations. Keep it simple; don't try to do too much. Ask ten to twenty sensory questions. You can do this exercise fifty times a day with fifty different objects. It allows you to work for the imaginary elements shortly after you experience the real stimulus. As you practice it over a period of time, you collect more and more objects to be used in the future. It also releases you from having to do a complete Sense Memory exercise every time you decide to practice.

Overall Sensation
This exercise involves your whole body. Submerge yourself in a bathtub or pool and sensorially investigate your physical and tactile responses. Try to re-create them after you leave the tub or pool. Do the same thing when you lie in the sun, whether in a backyard or on a hot, sandy beach, and re-create it later.

Now that you have the tools to work with, invent other exercises for yourself.

SENSORY INVENTORY

Once you approach a state of BEING—that point at which you are experiencing everything you are feeling, expressing all your impulses, doing no more nor less than what is, and being comfortable doing it—the next step is to determine what it is that you *want* to feel. That is, what does the scene obligate you to feel? Once you have explored and found the specific obligations, then decide which one you will work toward. Long before you take on the responsibility of a scene, however, you should involve yourself in craft homework. Since you must play the scales before you perform the concerto, let's explore "playing the scales" in more depth. Try a Sensory Inventory, isolating each sense and working with them one at a time:

The Tactile Sense
Find out where in your hand you feel, and why. You will discover that there is more sensation in some parts than others. Take a pencil and gently run it from the tip of your finger to the wrist. You will notice distinct differences in tactile response. For example, you probably feel less just below the fingernail than on the pads of your fingers. The reasons is that there are more nerve endings in the pads. There is also more response in the fingertips than in the second joint. Take another object, such as a matchbook or coffee cup, and move it along the insides of your fingers, along the back of your hand. Touch it to your cheek and to other parts of the body. You will find out many things about the *tactile* sense, such as the fact that the parts of the body that are covered with clothing are move sensitive to temperature and texture than the exposed parts.

Try holding an ice cube in the palm of your hand and see how long it takes for your hand to acclimate to the cold. Be aware of the changes that occur. Work with a variety of textures (cloth, wood, metal, etc.) and really allow the tactile sense to investigate them. Be sure that you ask yourself many questions about your responses—such as why you feel more in one place than another. Determine which parts are more responsive to shape, texture, temperature, and other factors.

The Olfactory Sense
Now try exploring your sense of smell. Fill a tabletop with a variety of objects that have a decided odor: perfume, a chocolate bar, a lemon, a can of coffee. Sniff each one, and go back and forth between the odors. By sniffing deeply you will discover that, as the odors penetrate, you actually smell more elements of that odor. If you watch a dog sniffing, you will observe that the dog throws the smell far back into its nose by sniffing deeply many times. Try to find out where in the nose smell actually

takes place. Block one nostril and sniff with the other to determine which nostril gives you the most response. Find out how far away you must move from the object before you begin to lose the odor. Ask many questions about the sense of smell so that you can explore it totally.

The Gustatory Sense

Try working with a piece of hard candy or some tasty liquid. Roll them around in your mouth and find out where and in how many parts of your mouth the sensation of taste actually occurs. In some parts you will experience bursts of flavor. Be aware that taste takes place in the roof of the mouth, the tongue, the cheeks, and the sides of the tongue. The lips and the teeth, on the other hand, respond to the shape and subtle textures of food and drink. Draw some air into your mouth and let it mix with a liquid, the way wine tasters do. The air will excite and increase your taste. By asking yourself a lot of questions, you'll discover where the tastbuds are, and how, when, and why they work.

The Visual Sense

When working with the visual sense, be aware that the eyes have a tendency to skip over many details and go to things that are interesting. Unless we train our vision to be specific, it will limit our perceptions to the overall object. If you look at an object, focus on it, and then quickly look away, you will experience an afterimage like the negative of a photo. Work with each eye separately, and note the differences and peculiarities of each one. You can explore dimension by holding a finger in front of your face and blinking one eye and then the other. Look at the texture of an object and then touch it, experiencing the difference between how it feels and what your eyes told you it might feel like. You might blindfold yourself and after a period of time, remove the blindfold to discover what a feast of colors, sizes, and shapes you see.

The Auditory Sense

The ears are conically shaped in order to trap sound, and people whose ears stick out from their heads usually hear better than those who have pinned-back ears. Try cupping your ears and see what happens. As you do so, talk and listen to your own voice. Play with music, turning the volume loud and soft. Isolate the individual sounds, turning your head in various directions. Try to break down sounds into vibrations, and determine how and where you hear. Sounds that emanate directly in front of you or directly behind you are hard to track in relation to direction and origin. If you plug your ears and listen, you will find that you can hear the sounds of your own body. Moreover, the body is very noisy: you can hear the pounding of your heart, the coursing of your blood, and the sounds you make swallowing, breathing, and digesting.

Finding out how your senses work is an exciting adventure. You become your own pathfinder, and the paths are infinite. Enjoy playing with your senses in all kinds of environments and with many kinds of objects.

SELF-INVENTORY

Self-Inventory, which is not to be confused with Personal Inventory or Sensory Inventory, is a process of taking stock of your life . . . your day, your month, the past year, a time five years ago, and so on. It's a recalling of the emotional events in your life, but most important, it is the *cataloging* of the *sensory elements* of those experiences. Then when you need the feelings later on in your work, you will know what buttons to push.

When I was a boy, I hated going to sleep at night. I would lie awake for a long time and make up stories, fantasize, and cast myself in any role I wanted. Thus I used this time to stimulate my imagination, and the habit carried on through the years. When I began to act, I switched from fantasizing to discovering new choices that I could use in scene work.

When you go to bed at night, start thinking about the day. What happened? What was significant? Whom did you see? Reconstruct the day sensorially. Try to remember the sounds and smells of things. Recall the objects around you, reexperience the way things felt in various parts of your body, remember what was said and how it was said.

Self-Inventory
Begin Self-Inventory by just going over a single day. Do it for a couple of weeks, and as you develop a facility for recall, go back a full week, pick out one day, and reconstruct it. Then go back a month, letting your mind wander from experience to experience. As your memory ranges over the months, you will find it easier to relate to a special day, like your birthday or Christmas. Use that important day as a base from which to work forward or back in time.

As you practice Self-Inventory you will recall more and more incidents from the past. People you had forgotten will jump into your memory, and along with their reemergence will come the thoughts and feelings you had about them. Encourage yourself to reexperience these feelings, and remember sizes, shapes, colors, and sounds. At first you may encounter some difficulty in going back into childhood. With practice, however, you will be amazed at how everything locked in your brain cells begins to surface.

Another way to do Self-Inventory is to keep a journal, a daily record starting today and recording all your significant experiences. Describe as many of the sensory stimuli and other elements of that experience as you can. A year or two from now you can look at your journal and find a fully drawn experience, complete with emotional responses. When you recall any incident, encourage yourself to reexperience the emotional response. Be careful not to make it a cerebral involvement.

Self-Inventory, practiced daily, will enlarge the repertoire of life experiences that you can use in your work. It will add dimension to your behavior on and off the stage.

ON-THE-SPOT EXERCISES

This book has discussed a multitude of acting obstacles—problems that keep you from functioning creatively. Many of them present themselves only when you are "on the spot"—onstage or in front of the camera. Nevertheless, you can practice certain exercises at home that will help you face the "demons" when they appear on the spot. A number of acting problems have their roots in tension and in the obligation to be good in the part. Listed below are several exercises you learned in earlier lessons. Use them to eliminate some of these problems.

Abandonment
Practice this when your tension is so great that the conventional relaxation groups do not work. It is a large-commitment exercise that you cannot do on a sound stage, since it would call unwanted attention to you. Simply yell, scream, rant, and rave with total Abandonment. Move your body with the same kind of abandon, so that you resemble someone having an uncontrollable tantrum. Your behavior should be formless, not logical or premeditated. Continue until you feel tired. It is best to lie on a soft surface and stay in a fairly small area, and since you are venting violent energy, be careful not to hurt yourself. Through the Abandonment exercise you can eliminate your tension and free a lot of emotions which were buried beneath that tension.

Miniabandonment
Use this version when you are forced to prepare on the set and you can't get off somewhere by yourself. Find a quiet corner if you can and, standing on your feet, express the same sounds less audibly. Violently tense and relax your body as you make the sounds. Although Miniabandonment doesn't have as strong an impact on your tension as the full-scale version, it can pull you through a tight spot.

Dump
If you are congested with anger or hostility, start expressing your frustrations, dissatisfactions, resentments, disappointments, needs, and desires in a large voice. Continue dumping until you achieve an eruptive flow of all that has been suppressed. "I'm tired of _____ . . . I can't stand _____ . . . I hate to _____ . . . I'm not going to stand for any more _____ . . . Nobody is going to tell me that I can't _____ . . . I'm sick of _____ . . ." When you are spent, you'll find that you feel free to go on to other things.

Yeah, Yeah!
To help yourself up from an emotional ''low'' to a high level of energy and ego, try Yeah, Yeah! Start using the word ''Yeah,'' and make it bigger and louder each time you say it. Pull it up from the soles of your feet. As you go along, you might add words: ''All *right* . . . Terrific . . . I feel fantastic!'' Use an enormous amount of physical energy to support your statements. You'll be surprised at how much excitement you generate. If you do the exercise in front of a group of people, they become excited too.

DAILY WORK: VULNERABILITY EXERCISES

A good way to keep track of the work you do each day is to keep a journal. List the exercises that you practice and comment on your progress in each area. Such a journal makes you more aware of your particular problems and gives you the feeling that you are building something.

It is essential to choose exercises for your daily work that make you accessible and ready to deal with objects and obligations. Be sure to train yourself in vulnerability.

Meaningful Sensory Choice
Imagine an object (a thing, person, animal, place, piece of music, or whatever) that you know has a significant emotional effect on you. Work for it by using Sense Memory. Ask questions that can be answered by the senses, and continue the process until the object exists and is affecting you.

Meaningful Imaginary Monologue
Talk to someone for whom you have strong feelings as if the person were here now. Discuss things that you feel are important and that arouse strong emotions in you. Allow the imaginary person to respond to what you say. Imaginary monologues can be a good means of becoming vulnerable.

Have a Fantasy about Yourself
Fantasize about something that thrills you, like receiving an award for your work. Imagine being given it and making a speech of acceptance. In my classes I use the Academy Award exercise, in which an actor stands in front of the class to deliver an acceptance speech. This exercise stimulates all kinds of emotional life in addition to vulnerability.

There are many things that you can do each day which will nurture you as an actor. Don't become a "short sprinter"—a person who works hard and fast for a day or two and then quits.

OBSERVING PEOPLE

For years I have been "people watching" with great interest and enjoyment. When I have a little extra time, which is rare, I go to an outdoor restaurant and observe the passing parade. And since I spend a lot of time in airports, I have the opportunity to watch a variety of travelers and scenes that are sometimes charged with theatrical emotion.

As an actor you should become a student of life and of people's behavior. You should be able to observe, understand, and learn from them and use your discoveries in your own work. It is important, however, to know the processes involved in observing people; you cannot just go out and watch them without knowing what you are looking for.

Observing People
Go where people congregate: parks, theatres, restaurants, buses, airports, zoos, banks, and many other places. (I used to take my classes to the Farmers' Market for people watching.) Try to observe unobtrusively, since people behave differently when they know they are being watched. At first try to "see" as much as you can. As you watch, constantly ask yourself "'Why?" People "wear" their life stories, and as you ask yourself questions, you will learn what to look for. Soon you will see much more than you ever realized you could.

Observation exercises train you to become involved in things outside yourself, instead of being limited to your own subjective concerns. They stretch your perceptions, and this increases your affectability: the more you perceive, the more you respond to. As you develop skill in observation, you will learn to isolate elements of human behavior and define their origins. Later when you are onstage, you can create stimuli that will produce similar behavior in you.

Start your observation by noticing how a particular person relates to everything around him or her. How is the person dressed? What does that tell you? How does the person relate to his or her body? Is the person aware of the environment, or self-involved? How does the person relate to this environment? Does the person notice other people? Some people function no further than six inches away from their faces and don't get involved with anything that demands a response. What does that tell you? Is such a person self-conscious?

People inadvertently point to their sensitivities and the things that they are anxious about. For example, the short person tries to overcome his shortness by standing to his full height. The very tall, lanky guy slumps out of self-consciousness. People who are embarrassed about their teeth often talk behind a concealing hand. Or they keep their top lip stiff so you can't see their teeth. A woman with acne scars will keep her face immobile in the mistaken idea that immobility will conceal it. You, the observer, can become expert in identifying self-consciousness and the various ways people attempt to handle it.

There is a technique I call *deductive observation,* which simply means trying to understand behavior by accumulating your observations and deducing a probable reason for it. Suppose that you are observing a man who is dressed in a business suit, carries a briefcase, and is reading a publication dealing with big business. A simple conclusion would be that he is a businessman, perhaps an executive of some company. You might wonder: ''Is he a minor executive, or does he hold an important position in the company?'' Go further with your observations: ''Is he dressed expensively, or are his clothes moderately priced? Are his clothes worn-out, or fairly new? How old is he? Does he have an air of self-importance? What jewelry is he wearing? Does it look expensive? How is he groomed? Is his hair styled, or is it just a haircut? Is he alone? If not, what kind of people is he with? How does he relate to the people around him? Does he behave as if authority comes naturally to him, or is his manner tentative?'' This kind of deductive observing will lead you to many conclusions, and often they are right. Of course, the man you were observing may be an unemployed actor who is selling real estate, but go ahead and take that chance. You have nothing to lose, and more often than not you will be accurate. The use of deductive observation will help you to see more, go deeper, and become more involved in the process of observing people.

A group of actors doing a Sense Memory exercise at a Marathon

THE MARATHON EXPERIENCE

Recently I conducted a two-day BEING and Craft Marathon in the mountains. Twenty-five people were there, and by the end of the second day every one of them had reached an inspiring openness and vulnerability. The communication was on the highest of levels, and as actors they were fully ready to work. The feeling of ensemble was compelling. If we had started to rehearse a piece, I am sure that the work would have been awesome.

How did twenty-five people achieve this state of BEING? For two long days we worked in instrumental areas, stripping away the inhibitions and demons each person had brought along. We also shared each other's process and became involved in the community effort of dealing with blocks and problems. We experienced each other's difficulties and breakthroughs, everyone's pain and pleasure in the work. At the end of that time, we all felt that we had a stake in each person in the room, and we felt that we had helped one another.

The big question is: How do you get the Marathon experience into your daily life and your acting? What can we as actors do by ourselves and in our work with other actors to reach a state of ensemble like that? One of the discoveries I made at the Marathon was that you must work together daily, sharing the process, giving and taking from each other.

Set up times with small groups to work together. Get away from competition and envy, and involve yourselves in the joy of exploration. I promise that you will be happier than you ever imagined, not to mention better prepared to act. Do exercises, do monologues; take the emphasis off being good and impressing each other.

When two actors are functioning on a moment-to-moment level, and everything each feels is being stimulated and affected by the other, they generate a level of excitement and reality that is electrifying. The way to achieve this phenomenon is to prepare to let it happen.

HOW

Most of the actors I have encountered, in either workshop or professional circumstances, cannot tell you specifically how they work. They can discuss general and abstract approaches, but when I ask, "How did you arrive at the life in the scene?" their answers are rambling and vague. Why can't actors explain how they act? I have been given a variety of excuses, such as "Acting is too complex; you're dealing with the human instrument." "There are too many variables." "It's not an exact science, you know!" Those responses are rationalizations for never having learned the *how!*

There is a *how,* and for many years it has been a crusade of mine to teach it. The simple fact is that if you know what to do and how to do it, you can do it *every time.* Furthermore, you can tell anybody how you do it. After every scene performed in my classes, I ask the actors, "What did you do? *How* did you do it . . . and why?" The actors who have learned their craft can tell you what they chose to work for, specifically how they worked for it, why they made the choice in the first place, and what life and realities they hoped to stimulate with their specific choice. The actors who have not mastered their craft give all kinds of answers:

"What did you work for?"
"Well, I worked for anger."
"No, you can't work for anger, since anger is the result of what stimulates it! Did you work for a choice that would make you angry?"
"I used my father."
"Oh, you worked for your father because he makes you angry?"
"Yes, that's what I did!"
"*How* did you work for that choice?"
"What do you mean, *how* did I work for him?"
"I mean *how* did you actually work to create your father?"
"I thought about him."
"Oh, do you always get angry when you think of your father?"
"Well, no, only when he acts a certain way!"
"Then you thought of him in a certain way?"
"Yes."
"And that made you angry the way the character in the scene is angry?"
"Yes!"
"Thinking about a person or other object only leads to a cerebral process and produces retrospective intellectual responses! Your father did not exist for you here in this room at this time, did he?"
"No, I only saw the other actor."
"If you were able to create your father so you could see him and hear and feel him, do you think that would have affected you the way the character is affected?"

''Yes, if he were really here in the room behaving the way he does when he makes me angry, I would feel exactly the way the character feels!''

''Well then, you must be able to create that reality through your craft process. *How* would you do that?''

''I really don't know.''

Other actors give similar responses:

''I worked for a sensory thing.''

''*How?*''

''I just did!''

''*How* did you work for the sensory thing?''

''I wanted to feel cold all over, so I imagined that I was cold all over.''

''That's not the same thing as really feeling cold, is it?''

''I don't know what you mean!''

What I am suggesting is that there is a process of work which will actually stimulate a sense of being cold. The actor will not just imagine it, but really *feel* it! You can learn *how* to create objects so they really exist for you here and now . . . *how* to create an environment so that you are really there . . . *how* to create your father, mother, wife, lover, child so that you can really see them and hear their voices . . . *how* to work on the stage so that you actually experience the inner organic life of the character. Once you know the *how,* no one can interfere with your ability to function. Your confidence and your self-worth will skyrocket, and you will be able to create in any environment, no matter how adverse.

What usually occurs is that the actor fools himself into thinking he is actually engaged in a process of work when in reality he is just adding to his burden by dealing in abstractions. He assumes behavior which is conceptual and believes that the life he is experiencing comes from this intellectualization. Unfortunately, he would be better off using nothing. The *how* that I speak of relates not only to craft but also to BEING. You must know how to prepare yourself instrumentally as well as in the craft area.

Actually, there are a lot of hows: *how* to prepare to act, *how* to recognize the specific problem or obstacle, *how* to eliminate tension, *how* to make choices in a scene, and *how* to work for those choices.

BEING, of course, is the necessary prelude to any creative process. To achieve that state, you must get in touch with what you feel at all times. *How?* Through Personal Inventory, Self-Inventory, Selfless Involvement, Abandonment, Observe, Wonder, and Perceive, and Stream of Consciousness. These exercises appear throughout the book.

Once you are ready to deal with the material, you must know the obligations: those elements in the material that you have to fulfill. The most important obligations in any scene are—
>Relationship to place and time
>(Where the character is, how he is affected by the place, and how the time of day, month, or year affects him.)
>Relationship to the other characters
>(What and how your character feels about the other people in the piece.)

Emotional obligations
(What he experiences emotionally in each scene.)
Character obligations
(Physical, psychological, intellectual aspects of the character.)
Thematic obligations
(What the author says through the character.)
Background and historical obligations
(What the character has experienced before the play and how it has affected
the way he behaves.)

In order to fulfill the obligations, you must first identify them. Read the material thoroughly, looking at the whole piece objectively. Do not allow yourself to be trapped by subjective involvement with the character you will play. Reading the piece will tell you where and when it takes place, what the author is trying to say, and any other existing character elements. The most important understanding of the obligations comes from:

1. What the author says about the character
2. What the other characters say about the character
3. What the character says about himself
4. The author's italicized descriptions of the character's actions and behavior.

Once you have a total understanding of what you must deal with, you can begin to approach the obligations *one at a time.* Suppose you choose to start with the place, because the environment in this particular play has a significant influence on the behavior of the character. He is stuck in his car in the desert; it's one hundred and twenty in the shade; and there isn't any shade. He, his wife, and two children are all tightly packed into the car, and the car is a compact.

Now that you know exactly what you will work, *how* do you work for it? There are many choice approaches, but in this instance you should use Sense Memory because the environment is particularly related to sensory elements like heat, cramped quarters, and the sounds of whining children. You might start by creating the heat first. To remind yourself *how* to do that, refer back to the Sense Memory exercises detailed in earlier lessons. Ask questions that related to each sense;

"Where on my face do I feel the temperature?"
"What does it feel like?"
"Where is it most intense?"
"As I breathe, what does the air feel like as it enters my nostrils?"
"What does the heat smell like?"
"Where on my face do I feel the density of the air?"
"How does the outside temperature differ from my body temperature?"
"What is heat in terms of what I feel?"
"What do I feel around my eyes? nose? mouth?"
"How does it affect my ability to breathe?"

Be specific and ask many, many questions. When you begin to feel the heat on your face, go to the rest of your body. If you have difficulty in this area, spend some time in a steam room at the gym and take Sensory Inventory there. After you have been successful at creating a sense of intense heat, deal with the other elements—the closeness of the cramped car, the wailing of the children, and so on. If you approach the scene through this process, you will be delighted at the emotional life that it produces.

After you establish the place, find a choice to work on for character. Suppose that you decide on a specific person in your life, because this person makes you feel just the way the character feels. What then? The person may no longer be a part of your life, or may be three thousand miles away. Do you just ''picture'' the person? ''Imagine'' that he or she is here? ''Pretend'' that you see the person before you? Too general! What's more, this procedure rarely works to stimulate your belief, since it stimulates only the intellect and not the emotions. Instead, create the choice sensorially so that you can really see it, hear it, feel it, smell it. *How* do you do that? Through a knowledge of Sense Memory, which also has a specific *how* attached to it. Or you can try an Imaginary Monologue, and that also carries a *how*. This is an almost foolproof way to find out whether you actually know what you are doing, or whether you're spinning your wheels with busywork. With every approach you make to a part, ask yourself *how* you plan to arrive at the reality. If you delude yourself into believing that you know how when you don't, you are costing yourself valuable time. Put yourself on the spot; ask—

What do I want to feel?
How do I make make myself feel that way?

WORK IN PROGRESS

What do you think would happen to the creative process if you always had to turn in a finished performance that was good, exciting, and theatrical? How do you think you would arrive at your desired creative results if you could not experiment and explore? To achieve organic realities, you need a place where you can fail—a place that you can use for your work in progress. Most important, this should be a place where you can receive productive criticism. Countless actors go to classes and workshops every week and hear compliments about their talent; but easy praise, or even generalized fault-finding, is counterproductive to growth. There are a lot of elements that contribute to the misuse of time, and the serious actor must recognize them as obstacles. Some of these obstacles are obligations you place on yourself, while others are related to the expectations of the other people in class.

It all depends on the way a class or workshop is structured. Some classes emphasize a finished scene complete with props and costumes. These are not helpful! Neither is criticism that puts value judgments on your work, such as "I thought you were very good," "That was bad work," or any comments that do not further your understanding of what you are doing and what you could do next.

Some actors and directors use the phrase "work in progress" as a copout for failure to accomplish their goals. Properly understood and used, however, a work in progress simply means that you are approaching a piece of material systematically and attempting to fulfill all the realities. It means that you are trying different choices and allowing yourself to BE the way the choices affect you, even at the risk of being dull and tedious. It means using workshop time for the reasons that we have workshops in the first place. It means having the courage to deal with people who do not understand what you are doing or why you are doing it. It means taking chances and exposing your impulses even before you know what those impulses are. It means being confused and blocked, and stumbling around searching for truths. In short, it means claiming your time and space to explore your craft.

Once in my class Joan Hotchkis, a talented actress, went onstage to work with a piece of material that she had written, It was the first time that she had dealt with the material publicly, and I'm sure she felt in double jeopardy. Joan, who was my coauthor on the book *No Acting Please,* has been an established actress for many years, and she had the right, if anyone does, to feel that there was something at stake and that she had to be "good." But instead, she dealt with her demons openly, allowed us to see all her obligations to be "good," acknowledged her moment-to-moment life, and used her time creatively and with great courage. When she had problems, she included that life in the framework of the material. Her attitude toward both the class and her work was positive and open. When she finished the piece I criticized her work, and she received my suggestions without ego or image protection. She was eager to accept what I saw, and she immediately related it to *how* she could deal with specific problems. We did a little work following the critique, and I could see her immediate application of what we had discussed.

Joan's was really "work in progress," not a form of lip service to a fine-sounding phrase. If you are interested in art and the creative process, then you go to class for the right reasons. You do not demand that the other actors provide an entertaining evening! Think about it.

USING REHEARSALS

Supposedly, the purpose of rehearsals is to explore material and a variety of choices for a character, as well as the actor's relationships to people, time, and place. But actors unfortunately often see the rehearsal as a cumulative performance and try to be "better in the part" with each successive attempt. That approach leaves no room for experimentation and failure, and the actor is in a rut.

The reason for such a misuse of rehearsal time is most often related to the fear of failure. No one wants to be bad or to be ridiculed, so actors develop a complex system of mannerisms that they use from play to play. These superficial mannerisms block the connection between the impulses arising inside the actor and the expression of those impulses.

To use rehearsals creatively, assign yourself a task to deal with in each session. The following is an example.

> In the first rehearsal I am going to read the script with a stream-of-consciousness approach, allowing myself to say the author's words from my own moment-to-moment reality. I will not concern myself with meaning or interpretation, and I will allow myself to be totally "irreverent" toward the material. By doing so I will not form any concepts about the part or the obligations; therefore I will leave myself open to discovering more elements in the material.

> In the second rehearsal I will isolate a single obligation, one that deals with what the character is feeling in the scene (the most important emotional obligation in the scene). Then I will ask myself how and what would make me feel and behave that way. After deciding on a choice and a choice approach, I will begin to work for the choice and at the same time encourage the author's words to come from the moment-to-moment life that is going on within me. I will improvise the scene or paraphrase the words so as not to get trapped by the logic or meaning of the words too early in the rehearsal. If there is time left over, I will tackle another obligation or character element, and if there is no time I will approach that in the next rehearsal.

> In every rehearsal I will be true to my own feelings and include them in everything I do. When a problem occurs I will deal with it in rehearsal and not sweep it under the carpet.

A good technique while rehearsing is to keep an inner monologue going. This technique adds dimension to your behavior and color to the character. Rehearsing is like building a house: you lay the foundation and add to the structure each day until it is a house.

FREEDOM TO EXPLORE

One night in my class when two actors were doing a scene, it was obvious that they had problems with each other and were trying hard to function in spite of them. The problems I refer to are the problems the characters in the scene had with each other. These characters, a man and a woman involved in a romantic relationship, were unhappy with themselves, each other, and their lives, but were surviving and functioning in spite of everything. The scene had progressed about five minutes when the actor rose from his chair, put on his jacket, and announced to the actress that he was leaving. Then he walked out, with her following on his heels. The scene ended a full ten minutes early. Afterwards, I asked the actors what they were working for, how and why. I also asked the actor why he had ended the scene prematurely. He said "I just couldn't be there with her anymore. She was bugging me, and I had to get away from her and that place."

This was what the character had felt, and felt intensely. However, if he left the stage every night when the emotional atmosphere became too heavy, the actors would never get through the play. We all laughed and agreed that somehow, in spite of the actor's level of reality, he must make some adjustment that would keep him there. The important point is that in a laboratory situation he did what he was impelled to do. Had he inhibited his impulse to leave, he would have short-circuited all the life behind that impulse. The solid achievement was that both actors had established a level of reality that led them to feel the depth of the relationship.

A workshop is a place to experiment, a place to take chances, explore, fail, discover. There are places where that actor would have been reprimanded for lack of professionalism, and such a rebuke might have severely damaged his spirit of exploration. Repeated reprimands make actors cautious and result in conventional, predictable acting. The actor who walked out must find a real reason to stay in a performance situation, no matter how much he wants to leave. In that framework, he can allow his feelings their own expression.

Art needs freedom. There must be a place where the actor is encouraged to do his work and not have to be good. You must try many things in order to find the stimulus that creates reality. Have the courage to follow your choices until you decide to use them or abandon them. If you are conservative in exploring your craft, you will do conservative work.

ACCEPTING CRITICISM

Once in my class when the students and I gave a critique of two actors' work, both of them were upset and hurt. It was so painful for them to listen to what was being said that they missed the salient points of the criticism. They responded as if they were being personally attacked, as if they were being judged as people and found valueless.

Naturally when something is as important as acting is to actors, a lot rides on doing well and being good. Nonetheless, in order to grow as an artist, it is essential to separate your ego from your work. If these actors had done that, they would have heard some helpful pointers that could be used the next time they approachd the scene. How many times have you lost your objectivity and responded to a director's criticism as if he were wounding you? I have more than once. And when you are working on a movie set where you have no time to recover, you ''go under'' and somehow just manage to get through the shot or the day. It is a miserable experience—and one that can be avoided.

What can you do to remain objective and open to criticism? Unfortunately, you cannot change just by deciding to. You must help yourself to become involved in the means and not the end. There is so much emphasis placed on talent and how much you have, and so much worry spent on whether people will see it or not. Talent is cheap and, contrary to what most people think, not very rare. What is rare is the *development* of that talent. Working on your instrument and on a process that allows you to make the most of it is the way to get your ego out of the center of things. The next time someone criticizes your work and you begin to feel hurt or defensive, stop and ask yourself: ''Is there anything I hear that can help me to function better?'' People have eyes and ears, and their responses must not be discounted. Take everything you can get from any place you can get it—and use it! When you are told how good you are and how wonderful the scene was, of course it makes you feel great. It is more valuable to your craft, however, to listen to constructive criticism and put it to work.

ART VS. FACILITATION

Some very gifted facilitators have spent many years perfecting their ability to represent life on the stage without really experiencing a single emotion that the character feels. They present behavior in the form of convincing line readings, and they repeat dialogue until it pleases their ear. The organic actor, on the other hand, works and often struggles to create the emotional life of the character internally. The major difference in results is that the facilitator stretches his audience into supplying their own realities and in a sense doing the acting for him, while the organic actor really experiences the life and shares that experience with his audience. It is the difference between a fine painting and a cartoon: one is art and the other isn't. The tragedy is that the facilitator spends just as many years in learning how to perfect his imitations as the organic actor does in learning how to create realities.

Because the representational actor imposes behavior, his real emotional life goes on underneath that behavior, which means that he is always split. The audience cannot technically identify this split, but they can perceive it as a lack of authenticity in the actor's work. Even in life, when a person is split between what he is expressing and what his internal experience is, we respond to it as insincerity. To eliminate splits, one must always express the moment-to-moment life. In order to do that, you must root yourself in the belief that acting, like life, comes from truth. Begin searching for your truth, and be willing to work arduously on eliminating the obstacles to that truth. Once you have the proper orientation, it is really much easier to function honestly than it is to be presentational. Nothing is so agonizing to an actor as to know that he's faking, and nothing is so pleasurable as to experience the fullness of reality, complete with all the emotional colors of the rainbow.

Unfortunately, facilitation is widely accepted in our industry. It is promoted by scores of directors who haven't the foggiest idea of what a creative process is. These unschooled and untrained directors present tremendous obstacles to the organic actor by their insensitivity to preparation and work process. It takes a highly skilled craftsman to overcome their ignorance, to create in terms of them and in spite of them. If I had one wish, I would wish for a world where actors and directors were required to have years of organic training and years of apprenticeship working in collaboration with each other. This training would be devoted to the development of the uniqueness of each individual. The emphasis would be on reality and not cosmetic beauty. Such schooling would encourage loyalty to a specific craft process and dedication to art.

THE JOY OF PROCESS

Why do you act, or want to? Do you know? You should know. Is it because acting has always been glamourous and mysterious? Is it because you grew up watching movies and want to be like all your heroes? People have a number of reasons for dedicating their lives to acting. Often the reasons that bring you into it change after a while. It has been my experience that actors who want to act for the wrong reasons usually give it up in time, particularly if they are not successful.

The fulfillment in acting comes from the discovery of the joy in the creative process. Once you begin to taste the process and reap the rewards of your craft involvement, then you really understand why you act. There is a popular misconception that actors are lazy, but in fact it isn't the fear of work most actors suffer from, but the ignorance of process. As soon as an actor understands what to do and how to do it, a transformation takes place. At first comes the intellectual understanding, then a taste of craft success, then the joy of knowing that you have a finger on the handle. Soon an actor is doing a scene every week and spending six or seven hours a day working on his instrument and craft, when just a few months ago he could not muster the energy to do ten minutes of Sense Memory.

Have you experienced this joy that I speak of? "Oh, sure, yes I have," you say. But have you? I don't mean feeling wonderful in the middle of a performance, or getting carried away in a scene. We've all had those "great" experiences, and they are truly joyful, but few and far between. What I'm talking about is the real joy that comes from getting in touch with your true emotions, eliminating the obstacles that keep you from being comfortable with everything you feel, and reaching a state of BEING, where you do no more nor less than what you feel. You break the social shackles you have been bound by all your life, understand the process of creating realities on the stage, and know yourself well enough to make choices that stimulate an authentic emotional life in front of the camera.

When you discover this new world of process and fulfillment, you will begin to have new values and a new definition for the word success. Society judges success in terms of acceptance or money. You will consider a successful person one who does what he wants to do with his life and truly lives with the joy of his work.

ACTING: MORE THAN A JOB

"Acting is a job like any other job!" Has anyone told you that? Once I heard a famous actor compare it to being in the lumber business. In some ways it would very nice if acting were as steady and consistent as a regular business, but unfortunately it is not. Acting is more a way of life than a job, and if you love to act, it becomes a twenty-four-hour-a-day involvement. The training and practicing with your instrument should go on all the time, even at the unconscious level. If you work seven or eight hours each day, there is very little time left to be depressed or discouraged.

Everything that goes on around you should interest you. Observing and understanding behavior helps you as an actor to make the right kinds of choices to stimulate behavior on the stage. Understanding conflict, and the ways people function in terms of it, is crucial, since drama must contain conflict in order to be theatrical.

Besides observing the world, the actor must practice the creative techniques daily; Sense Memory, Affective Memory, dealing with choices, choice approaches, preparing material, and so on. Think of acting as an involvement that begins when you get up each morning and absorbs your entire day:

> At breakfast, do Sense Memory with your coffee.
> Practice Personal Inventory to find out where you are emotionally.
> Work for about an hour in sensitizing or vulnerability areas to make you more accessible.
> Pick an area of emotional life that you have difficulty in and work on it, exploring the kinds of things which might stimulate that life.
> Go out and people-watch.
> Go to the zoo and study animals. Bring your observations home and translate them into human behavior.
> If you are working on a scene or monologue, spend a few hours in the afternoon on that.

As you encounter difficulty, whether instrumental or craft-related, deal with it. You may run into blocks that take many days of work to eliminate. At the end of each workday, you will feel as if you have accomplished a great deal and are further down the road to being an artist. Don't sit around with other actors and bemoan your fate. Stay away from too much self-involvement; it is counterproductive and boring. Draw up a daily working schedule and stay with it. You will like yourself a lot more. Get together with other actors who want to work and find your fun in working!

WHY ACTORS AVOID DAILY WORK

What is it that keeps so many of us from either learning the craft or practicing the techniques that lead to creativity? The main reasons why actors have difficulty with discipline are the lack of immediate rewards and the solitary nature of daily practice. When an actor gets up in class and does an exercise, there is instant feedback. He experiences a rush of excitement similar to that which occurs when the curtain goes up onstage, and sometimes this becomes his sole motivation for attending class.

Another reason for avoiding the craft process is the fear that you might not be able to do it. ("What if I spend months or years at this and then it doesn't work?") And of course, some actors avoid daily practice because of the tedium. But whatever the reasons, I promise you that the only way to become an artist is to learn your art. Whenever you see an actor who excites you, remember that he or she spent years, and tens of thousands of hours, perfecting those abilities. There is no way around doing the work, but there is a wonderful solution to the problem: Fall in love with the process! When you really become involved with the work, hours seem like minutes and the creative process becomes enchanting.

There are ways to make the work fun and ways to use it in your everyday activities, and when you taste that first solid response in a scene, you'll be hooked. You can spend your time avoiding your responsibilities as an artist, or you can accept those responsibilities. In either case, the years will pass and at the end of them, you will be bankrupt in your craft, or you will have an enormous creative "bank account."

MAKING THE WORK ENJOYABLE

There are a lot of actors in the world, and a lot of them study, but very few of them become master craftsmen. Why is that? Is it because talent is so rare? I think not. It is because most people are in it for the "brass ring" . . . being famous and loved and wealthy. I think all those things are wonderful! They are not, however, the essential ingredients of art. The element that must be present before you can become a creative artist is joy in the process of creating.

I have taught thousands of actors, and very few of them ever got beyond the tedium of doing a Sense Memory exercise. "It's dull, Eric; it's a bloody bore, and I run out of questions!" "It's really hard to sit through, and it's even harder to see how it will help me as an actor." It *is* difficult to sit and work on your craft for hours with on one there to applaud or appreciate your efforts. It is tedious if it isn't fun—but it can be!

Provided that you can get over your intense concern with results, there is a world of pleasure in all parts of the creative process. Discover the joy of being able to re-create an object so that you can see it, feel it, smell it, and taste it, when it isn't really there. In order to reach that point you must discipline yourself to do the work—and must look for ways to make it an adventure! You can find excitement in anticipating a rehearsal so that you can try some of the choices you have been working on. You can feel challenged by your obstacles and by the process of dealing with them through the hundreds of tools available to you. Understanding the work intellectually is only the beginning; you must be able to *do* the work. The only way that you can is to:

1. Find the *joy* in the process.
2. Work for *you*.
3. Discover your *passion* for acting.

We all want to see the finished canvas, but that is a trap that can keep you from using your time properly. Each time you rehearse or do an exercise, deal with only one element at a time. If, for example, a scene has many emotional obligations, break them down and approach them one by one. Know what it is that you want to feel, find a choice which you think will make you feel that way, and work for it until it does or doesn't. It's fine to spend two or three rehearsals dealing with one obligation.

Experiment—and enjoy your work!

MORE FUN WITH THE WORK

Acting should be fun! Having a good time can be difficult when you are dealing with problems and obstacles, but there are ways to lighten the load. For example, if you are working with Sense Memory and the exercise begins to seem tedious, ask yourself questions that stimulate whimsy: "If this cup of coffee could speak, how would it sound?" "If it had personality, what would it be like?" You can suggest a myriad of things in relation to your sensory objects that will amuse or entertain you. The same is true when you are working with choices for scenes. A good rule to follow is that when you get a little grim and start avoiding your work, it's time to find the fun again.

When you are working with another actor, you can trick or surprise him or her within the framework of the scene. Break your pattern of behavior and do things that are totally unexpected by both of you. Besides stimulating a sense of fun, this technique keeps you from falling into predictable behavior. It encourages expression of your moment-to-moment life and keeps the scene fresh. Doing improvisations that parallel the material can be fun. Approaching the scene in gibberish not only keeps you away from narrowly linear concepts but is very enjoyable. Working with fantasy helps the imagination and is a good way to have fun. When you are dealing with a piece of material, you can have a fantasy surrounding the circumstances of the scene, or you can create a fantasy that does not relate to the material at all. The whole area of fantasy piques the child in us all, and because it does, doors are opened that add dimension to a scene. Also practice large-commitment exercises that are fun: Superman, Yeah! Yeah! and Silly Dilly, for example.

The greatest sense of fun comes when you are working well and experience an inner organic life that flows freely. There is nothing so satisfying as BEING, and carrying that state into everything you do.

TAKE THE CHANCE OF DOING NOTHING

Everybody talks about the need for you to take chances onstage! On the set! In your life! Well, what does it mean? It means a lot of different things . . . It means to be adventurous with the kinds of choices you use . . . It means expressing the life you feel, instead of leading yourself to conceptual imposition . . . It means allowing yourself to trust your moment-to-moment impulses . . . It means to trick and surprise yourself . . . It means to run the risk of failing.

But the chance-taking I am talking about here is related to that moment in a scene when the actor feels an emptiness, feels that there is *nothing* there, that he is about to be dull and boring! At that exact moment where panic threatens to take over, most actors sell themselves out. They don't have the courage to do *nothing,* so they manufacture behavior to fit the material. And when they do that, the reality they may have created is short-circuited. The flow of organic impulses is stopped, and what usually happens is that the next twenty minutes of work is not real.

So what is to be done? When I tell an actor to trust himself and do no more than what he or she feels, I hear, "But I have an obligation to the audience and to the play!" Yes, you do, and that obligation is to be real and colorful and unpredictable—to BE what you are. An actor is not an imitator of life. He should be *the instrument through which impulses are created and expressed.* The resulting life is fresh and real. It fulfills the author's intent even while the actor brings to the stage the individuality that only he possesses.

That "moment of truth" when the actor in a scene feels an emptiness is very important to understand. It is not enough to tell him that he must have courage and do nothing at such a time. If you can grasp the idea that "nothing" is really many things, it will be easier to accept those terrifying gaps in the flow of your emotions. When you come up to that split second of nothingness, allow yourself to BE! Say the words of the scene from whatever you are feeling or not feeling. Or if at the moment you have no lines, allow yourself to relate to the other person or the environment from the experience of whatever is really happening to you.

Those so-called moments of nothingness are rich with thoughts and impulses that can be seen by an audience. The subtleties of reality are complex and delicious. Even if you don't feel their existence, they are there, and to deny them is an anticreative action that costs you dearly. The very next time you come upon one of these moments, try doing "nothing." Allow yourself to BE, and see what happens.

Take the chance!

DEALING WITH A DIRECTOR'S QUEST FOR RESULTS

A great number of directors ask for results. They tell you where to move and generally block the scene. They blueprint your emotions and expect you to fulfill their wishes. Dealing with "result" direction is hard even for a master craftsman, and for a less experienced actor it is almost impossible not to fall into the trap of playing out concepts. Here's an example of result direction:

Director: *All right, I want more anger at the beginning, and as you see her back down . . . get softer. On the line "That's better," go to her and touch her cheek. When she doesn't give you a warm response, go back and sit behind the desk.*

With those restrictions, the director should play the part himself. It is very difficult to stimulate a creative flow of impulses when you're thinking about every gesture and emotional response.

What can you do when you encounter such a director? *Interpret his demands in craft terms.* Listen to what he is calling for and ask yourself what choices you can make that might stimulate the moment-to-moment life within you. Don't simply panic and impose the behavior you think is necessary. Break down the obligations and find out what would make you feel the way you must in order to do what the director wants. Work for the choices, and see where they lead you. If what you work for doesn't stimulate exactly what you want, don't abandon the choice and impose the behavior; try something else.

While you are doing your work, you must stand your ground as an artist. Don't let a director or anyone else push you around; take your due and demand the time you need for your creative process. Tell him that you are trying to give him what he wants, but that you must create the realities which will support the actions. You sell yourself out if you don't do just that—and *you* take the rap, not him. Moreover, copping out can become a habit, and as you allow more and more imposed behavior to creep into your work, it becomes impossible to work creatively. Actors who do that support their faintheartedness with rationalizations: "You can't be creative in television; there isn't enough time." "They won't let you be an artist! And who cares, anyway? Say the jokes, take the money, and run." These are just lies that actors tell themselves in order to feel better about not doing what they know they should be doing. Every piece of work you take on is important, even if it is one line. If you maintain your integrity throughout your creative life, you will end up a winner!

PREPARATION AND PRE-PREPARATION

I've been telling you that ninety-five percent of acting is being prepared to act. However, the word *preparation* is like a continent which has many regions. To know how to choose the proper preparation is linked with knowing yourself.

Your daily practice is a kind of preparation that helps you to sensitize and solidify certain craft and instrumental techniques. BEING exercises keep you in touch with your personal reality and the moment-to-moment life you must get to before you can deal with any scene obligation. Acting is a total involvement, and you should be observing and absorbing constantly.

Start your preparation with the relaxation group of exercises. Once you are relaxed, sensitized, and in touch with the way you feel here and now, ask yourself what kind of pre-preparation you need in order to start preparing to do the scene. Depending on where you are emotionally, you could choose from any areas. Let us assume that the emotional obligation in the scene is to feel happy and free, with an overall sense of well-being. At this point you are in touch with your BEING state, and you feel congested and somewhat anxious. A good pre-preparation might be a large-commitment exercise such as Abandonment, Dump, Yeah, Yeah! or any of the others that act as an emotional expurgation. Then once you have done the pre-preparation, take a Personal Inventory and see if you are ready to go toward the scene preparation.

THE WHAT, WHERE, HOW, AND WHY OF CHOICES

Preparation is the greatest part of getting ready to get ready, but once you are ready to deal with the material, what then?

What is a choice?

Where do choices come from?

How do you work for them?

What are the right choices for the scene?

How do you find choices?

The word "choice" simply describes the object, the person, the sound, the place, or whatever you attempt to recreate that might stimulate the feelings you want for the scene. For example, a choice can be a photograph that makes you feel nostalgic. In this case your choice is either the real picture or a re-creation of it through sensorial work. A choice can be a piece of music that you work to re-create in order to fulfill the material. Choices come from you—from your living experience and the knowledge of what affects you. They come from your past and from the present.

There are a number of ways to approach working for a choice, but the most basic is Sense Memory. The right choice for a scene is the choice that will stimulate the character's emotional life and point of view. In order to make the right choice for a piece of material, you should explore several of them that may take you where you want to go.

After you have spent some time using a variety of choices, catalog a good number of them for future use. Choices are found by taking inventories of times and periods in your life and finding the impetus that caused certain things to happen emotionally. A daily awareness of how things affect you will build a storehouse of choices. Keeping a daily journal will be invaluable as you go back and pick out the stimuli that influenced your behavior.

OBLIGATION AND CHOICE

A good daily working schedule starts with instrumental preparations, proceeds to Sense Memory practice, then moves to exploration of choices. If you are working on a scene, you might experiment with a few different choices to see where they lead. If you are not preparing a scene, it's good practice to read several pieces of material and explore the various obligations. For the sake of learning and using your craft, identify the specific obligations in each piece and make choices that might lead you in the direction of fulfilling the obligations. Practice like this helps you learn to search for, find, and work for a variety of choices. When you are in a professional situation, you will have the ability and confidence stemming from that daily commitment.

To redefine choice and obligation: The *obligation* in a scene (and there are many) is that which you want to feel or reach. It is the emotional life of the character. The *choice* is what you work for in hopes that it will stimulate the desired emotional life.

You will explore many choice areas while working on scenes, and often get stuck without the right choice when you need it most. As suggested in the previous lesson, keep a daily journal reviewing the important happenings of each day. Talk about a specific experience you have had and describe it in as much sensory detail as possible: the sounds and odors related to the place, the size, colors, shapes, and textures of things. Discuss the way you felt, and specify the objects that made you feel that way. If your experience included other people, tell how they were dressed, what they talked about, and how their voices sounded. A month or a year from now, that experience might be just the choice you need for a scene.

Remember the exercise in an earlier lesson that asked you to review the day, week, month, and year each night before you went to bed. Choose experiences from these reviews to describe in your journal. Form the habit of taking a quick inventory any time something occurs that you might be able to use later as a choice.

You must also learn how to translate the experiences that you catalog into usable choices. Suppose that you decide to explore a time when you waited in the park for a person you loved who was very late. At first you felt excitement and anticipation, but as you waited, your excitement turned to anxiety and then to anger. How do you work for this choice in order to reexperience the same emotions?

Start with the sensory elements, and ask all the sensory questions in the present tense: "What color is the sky?" and so on. If you relate to that time as having been in the past, you can only hope for a retrospective emotional response and not a fresh experience. Now begin: What do you see in the direction that you are facing? How does the bench you are sitting on feel at first? How does it feel after you have been sitting for a long time? Work for the sounds of the park, the people, the birds and animals. Experience the weather, the temperature, the colors, and the light. Is it a sunny or a gray day? What are the clouds like? How are you dressed, and how do those clothes feel? From which direction do you anticipate the person's arrival, and how do you imagine that he or she will look? As you wait, how does the light change? Does the temperature change and affect your comfort? What things make you aware of waiting?

Work with choices as often as you can. Soon you will find that there are hundreds more than you suspected.

OUTLINE FOR OBLIGATION AND CHOICE

Stanislavski said that an actor must live the part, and there has been much misunderstanding about that statement. "Become the character!" What does it mean? Can you in reality ever be anyone else? The answer is NO! You can only be what and who *you* are, and that's as it should be. Living the part and becoming the character both mean that you experience similar emotions, have similar impulses, and relate to the world in a similar way. The playwright tells you who the character is, what motivates his behavior, how he feels about the other people in the play, and esssentially what his sense of life is. The author also tells you something of the character's history, background, and motivation—why that person does the things he or she does. This is your blueprint, the information you need to start your creative process.

I give my students an outline to follow, questions to ask themselves in an attempt to define the obligation and the choice:

> What does the person in the scene feel?
> What makes the character that way?
> What would make me feel that way?
> How can I apply that choice in this scene?

Your responsibilities go much further than the duty to stimulate organic emotion on the stage. Often an actor will say to me, "But Eric, it was real; I felt every moment." "Yes it was," I say, "but what about the entire fabric of the character's existence? What I saw was Joe feeling upset and angry. I saw Joe really experience those emotions, and I believed that you really felt those things, but the character has just been released from prison for a crime he did not commit. He spent years confined and mistreated, and now the people around him are prejudiced and rejecting him. Do you think that he is *just* angry and upset? Are you filled with the bitterness of his injustice? Have you been confined for a long period of time and been helpless to make anyone believe your innocence? Are you hurt as he is hurt? Has your life and everything you ever wanted been taken from you? Did you lose your wife because of the imprisonment?"

Joe says that he has never been in prison and has never been married. I ask him if he has ever had an experience that was unjust. He remembers a crushing time in high school when he was unjustly dismissed from the basketball team. He was rejected by the team members and all the people in school. He talks about the trauma of the experience and says that he felt as if the world had collapsed around him. I tell him to approach that whole experience through Affective Memory (described in detail on page 129) and see where it takes him.

It is not enough to work for choices that give you emotions similar to the character's. You must find in your own life experience the parallels that will help you to construct the entire fabric and inner emotional life of the character.

HOW TO APPROACH THE MATERIAL

When you get a part in a play, television show, or film, *how* do you approach it? What are the steps that you take in reading, understanding, and exploring the craft obligations of the material?

Make sure to read the entire piece so that you know how the scene relates to the overall material.

When reading, make a note of whatever is said about your character—by the author, by the character, and by the other people in the piece.

Every bit of information you get from the piece helps you to identify the obligations you will have to deal with:

        The emotional obligation
        The obligation to time and place
        The relationship obligations
        The character obligation (psychological, physical, emotional, etc.)
        The historic obligation (dealing with the time period)
        The thematic obligation (the author's statement through the character)
        The obligation to the style of the piece

There is a chronological order, differing with each piece, that you should follow when you attempt to deal with the obligations. For example, the emotional obligation in a scene may be strongly influenced by the nature of the character obligations. If the character is highly suspicious or even prone to paranoia, that tendency affects his relationships with the other characters and all his emotional behavior.

Once you understand the obligation that you want to work toward, look for the choice that might take you there. ''What do I want to experience, and what do I think will stimulate that kind of life?'' There are thousands of choices and a variety of choice approaches. What you choose to work for should be something that you have faith in. Of course, in rehearsal you should try many choices and approaches. The more you use your craft the easier the process becomes. The structure of some scenes lends itself to one choice approach better than another. Don't forget that there is a *how* to work beyond memorizing your lines and assuming behavior.

TASK INVENTORY

As I gained experience as an actor, having done a couple of hundred scenes in class and almost a hundred plays, I developed a large repertoire of choices. Even so, there were times when I worked on a new piece and none of my existing choices filled the bill. Out of desperation I conceived a Task Inventory exercise that I have used ever since for myself and my classes.

Task Inventory
First identify the obligation: ''What do I want to feel? What is the inner emotional life?'' Clarify it so that it is completely clear to you.

Next ask yourself if you have ever felt that way. Recall an occasion when you had a similar emotional life, and ask yourself what elements in the experience caused you to feel that way. For example, suppose the obligation is to feel elated and filled with joy. You remember experiencing those emotions once when you received a telephone call informing you that you had been given a part you really wanted. Therefore the sensory elements are your home, the time of day, the objects in the room, and most particularly, the telephone and the person's voice telling you the news. The next step in the process is to find another experience that stimulated elation and joy. After thinking for a while, you might remember an occasion when you came off the stage and someone told you how wonderful you were.

Now you have two experiences to relate to; find the common denominator between them. In these instances, it is the fact that you were affected by something someone said to you. Now pick the strongest of the two choices and translate it into a workable approach. Sensorially translate the experience so that you can work for it in choice terms. If you have decided to use the first incident, sensorially re-create the room, the time of day, the objects in the room, the way you were dressed, the telephone, the person's voice, the words he used, and his specific style of speaking. By the time you have finished, you should reexperience the desired emotional life.

If you are still at a loss after you have done all the parts of this exercise, ask yourself, ''What *would* make me feel that way if it existed here and now?

CATALOGING YOUR DAILY EXPERIENCES

Everything that happens to you in the course of a day should be acknowledged, evaluated, and stored for future use in your work. A great number of experiences pass unnoticed and are forgotten, whereas they could be excellent future choices in your work. Previous lessons have advised you to go over the significant events of each day and note them in your journal, being sure to describe the environment and all the sensory elements leading up to the experience. For example:

> I was sitting at a table in an outdoor restaurant. It was warm, and the sun cast shadows of the objects on the table against the wall nearest me. I was dressed in jeans and a T-shirt, and I could feel my perspiration under my shirt. The smells were a mixture of food and gasoline fumes from the passing cars. I felt lazy and undirected, and then I saw HER sit down at the next table. I couldn't take my eyes off her. She was beautiful—she reminded me of every woman I'd ever loved, and then some. I began to sweat heavily, and my heart was beating much more rapidly than before. I thought to myself that this was ridiculous, and yet I couldn't do anything about it.

And continue on, into the rest of the experience. When you look back at your journal a month or a year from now, that experience, replete with the description, might be the very thing you need for a scene. Another good way to save such events is to carry a small tape recorder with you whenever you go and note your experiences verbally. As a matter of fact, this technique is even better than keeping a written journal, since later you will be able to recapture emotions from the tone and texture of your voice.

In addition to cataloging your daily experiences, always be aware of what you are feeling and whether or not you are functioning in relation to what is going on. Being an actor carries with it responsibilities for constant search and discovery.

CHOICE APPROACHES

The choice is what you work for in order to stimulate the emotional life to which you are obligated by the material. A choice can be a place, an odor, a person, an inanimate object, or an animal. You work for the choice both during rehearsals and in the actual performance. The more choice approaches you have, the richer you are as a craftsman. Here is an overview of choice approaches—of the various ways to create realities.

Sensory Choice
Everything that you experience comes in through one or more of your five sensory doors. So what is meant by *sensory choice* is sense memory involvement. You work with the sense memory process to re-create an object that is not really there, to reproduce it so that you can see it, feel it, hear it, taste it, smell it. If you are successful at re-creating the object through sense memory, you can expect that it will stimulate an emotional response.

Imaginary Monologue
The imaginary monologue can be used in many ways: as a preparation, as an ego exercise, and as a choice approach in stimulating emotional life. Simply talk to any person in your life, past or present—particularly a person for whom you have strong feelings. Start by talking to the person as if he or she were there, saying things that you know will evoke emotional responses. Allow your imagination to supply the imaginary responses from the person. It is important to creatively lead yourself to areas that are emotionally affecting.

Believability
You and another actor can work together to explore Believability as a choice approach. It is accomplished by mixing very little truth with a lot of untruth, and choosing to believe everything. Suppose you are doing a scene in class with another actor. You might start a Believability exercise by saying, ''Why weren't you at the rehearsal this morning? I waited for two hours, and you didn't even bother to call!'' The other actor might reply, ''I'm really sorry I overslept. I had a bad night . . . Joe and I broke up!'' And so on and on until a group of emotional realities is taking place. In this example the *only* true fact is that the two actors are doing a scene together. It is important that you feed each other responses that promote Believability. This approach is rich in creative elements, and heightens your ability to believe in real things. Actually, the best Believability exercise in the world is a Sense Memory exercise.

Now we come to *how* you go about looking for the choice areas and, once you decide on a specific choice, *how* you translate it sensorially for use.

Betty involved in an Imaginary Monologue

WHAT ARE CHOICES?

Anything that affects you in life can be used as a choice in a scene. I use the word "object" to describe all choices. An object can be a person, thing, odor, sound, etc.

Here is a list of possible choice areas, to which you can add ideas of your own:
Photographs of important people or places
Letters of all kinds
Memorabilia—an autograph book, old clothes, an award you once received, dolls, toys
A love song you once shared with someone
Music popular when you were in high school
A place or a part of a place
People who have had an effect on your life
The smells of a place from your past
The taste of a food your mother used to prepare
Members of your family
A pet you once had

WHY USE CHOICES?

The choice is the object that you create in hopes that it will affect you emotionally and create thoughts, impulses, and behavior that are right for the material. Choices are also used to fulfill other elements of the material, such as obligations of characterization. Suppose that you are playing a person who lives much more on the basic animal level than you do—a person who moves and responds to the world more primitively. In this case you might use an animal as a choice and work to get a sense of that animal in your own body. This process of working to create a sense of animals is described in more detail later.

WHEN DO YOU USE A CHOICE?

Use a choice whenever you need to, but not when you don't. Often there is enough available reality to stimulate the life you want. In that case working for a choice would be like trying to start the engine of your automobile when it was already tooling down the highway at fifty miles an hour. Work for a choice when you need to stimulate emotions that you are not feeling at the moment; work for a choice when you want to change from one emotional level to another; work for a choice when you have to create any kind of reality for yourself.

HOW TO USE A CHOICE

The *how* depends on what choice approach you are using. If it is a sensory choice, for example, you approach it as a Sense Memory exercise.

Each choice approach has its own process and application. Your most important objective in working with a choice is to use your time properly. You must explore the choice in rehearsal, and while you do, your major involvement should be with the choice and not with the scene. Many actors try to work for a choice and at the same time express the meaning of the material, and they fail to do either. If you take the time to work for the choice, it will usually stimulate the desired life.

A good way to practice choice approaches is to set yourself a simple emotional obligation, making it very clear. Then select the choice and the approach and work on it. Get into the habit of doing this a couple of times a week.

Available Stimuli
Using the stimuli already available in your environment enormously simplifies your job of choice selection. Ask yourself: "How do I want to feel? . . . Is there anything in this place which could make me feel that way if I related to it?" Take the time to really explore your surroundings. If you do find an object that works, relate specifically to it by investigating it with questions: "How do I feel about that object? . . . What is my overall response? . . . With which of my senses do I relate the most? . . . What does it remind me of? . . . If I touched it, how would it feel?" Go on until you are experiencing the emotional life in the scene. You can do the same with other actors—look for available stimuli in them that will affect you the way you want to be affected.

Selective Emphasis
You may want to isolate an area of the meaningful object and relate only to that area. Suppose you are working with an actress or actor whom you like very much and in fact are somewhat attracted to, but the scene obligates you to a feeling of repulsion. Most actors automatically choose to work for someone else in relation to the person. If you really explore your partner, however, you might be able to isolate a small area or part of the person that you find unattractive. It could be something about the hair, the lipstick, or a separation between his or her front teeth. Or it might be a behavioral element or personality quirk. By using Selective Emphasis you identify the element, relate to it, and explore your feelings about it.

Creative Leadership

Start by using something that is really happening: ''She's smiling at me; I think she likes me, I can see that she is attracted to me. I think she would really like to get closer to me. I can see she is shy and probably afraid to take the next step, but I can tell how much she feels for me . . .'' You can go on with this as far as you like. Beginning with a simple smile, you have led yourself into the belief that this casual relationship is becoming the romantic dream of your life. As you progress your willingness to believe grows and it takes less and less leading to get you going. Creative leadership can also be used in Sense Memory by asking the kinds of questions that you know appeal to you sensorially and emotionally.

Evocative Words

Say words or phrases to yourself that relate directly to a meaningful experience you have had. Choose the words to outline the entire experience, and pay particular attention to those elements that will affect you. Choose the experience to match the desired emotional obligation. Say the words semiaudibly so that you can hear them. If you are doing a scene, of course, you cannot stand there mumbling to yourself, so say the words silently between the lines. The exercise should sound like this:

Sitting here, waiting . . . Nice office . . . Looks rich . . . Lot of people . . . Don't like waiting . . . Want this job . . . Need it desperately . . . She's pretty . . . Wonder how I look . . . Feel my stomach flopping around . . . Been here half an hour . . . Wonder what the script is like . . . Hope I can look it over . . . Tired . . . She came in after me! . . . That makes me angry . . . I'm nervous . . . Anxious . . . Wish this was over . . .

The example might have been chosen to restimulate the feelings you had in that office—the tension, need, and anticipation of the interview. By going through the experience in a kind of shorthand work excercise, you may reexperience emotions that you felt at the time. Evocative Words is a choice approach that works well most of the time, but be aware that it can lead to general responses that are not deep or organic. The way to avoid that trap is not to settle too early for the life that this exercise stimulates.

Elizabeth doing an Affective Memory as choice in a scene with Brad

Affective Memory

In order to use Affective Memory you must be skillful with Sense Memory. I recommend this complex process only for actors who have established themselves at a healthy level of craftsmanship. Affective Memory is the re-creation of a particular emotional experience—of a moment that had a strong impact on you. It should be an experience that took place approximately one to five years ago. More recent experiences, particularly painful ones, are hard to re-create because our own instruments work against us: our minds protect us from recalling painful areas. On the other hand, experiences from the distant past are hard to re-create because we forget a lot and important elements become vague.

Start the exercise by creating the environment where the experience took place. Suppose that you have chosen a moment when you walked out of a restaurant and saw a woman whom you had not met in many years stepping out of a taxi. You had been desperately in love with her and still felt strongly about her, and the impact of seeing her again was so great that you could never put it into words. Now this experience is exactly the kind of life you are after for the scene you are working on. How do you approach it?

Start back inside the restaurant. Ask sensory questions to re-create the surroundings in detail: the room, the size and shape of it, the decor, the colors, the furnishings, the wallpaper and wall hangings, the table, what was on it, the sounds in the room, the odors, the way you were dressed, the chair you sat in and how it felt, the people you were with, where they sat in relation to you and the room, the way they were dressed and the sound of their voices, the specific things you talked about, the temperature of the room, the time of night and the lighting of the room, the waiter and everything about how the food looked and tasted, the distance between tables and any conversation you overheard, other people in the restaurant and anything that you can specifically re-create about them.

Each of these things must be created in great detail, and *you must ask all sensory questions on a here-and-now basis.* Do not ask yourself what it was like, but what *is* the color of that wall, and how *does* the salt shaker feel to the tips of your fingers. If you ask the questions in terms of what was, you will accomplish only a retrospective response that will not lead you to the true here-and-now experience which Affective Memory is capable of.

Continue to re-create the events leading up to the moment when you came face to face with the woman. If you are successful in the process, then that moment may again have the total impact on you that it had the first time. Follow every step in the chronology so that you do not violate your own reality. Work for the conversation at the table, the decision to leave the restaurant, paying the bill, walking to the door, what you saw from that perspective, the cashier and how she was dressed, walking out into the night air, the adjustment of your eyes to the difference in light, the arrival of the taxi, the kind of car it was and its colors, the door opening, seeing her, how she first looked, the color of her hair, her eyes, what she was wearing, how she moved, specifically how she had changed over the years, what you remembered and what you had forgotten. All these responses take place in an instant, so you must be very specific in re-creating them.

When you first work on an Affective Memory, it may take hours; but with repetition the time required decreases until you can re-create it in minutes. The advantage of this approach is that it creates a multidimensional life filled with color and rich with unconscious impulses that are compelling to watch. In some cases it is the only way to pique an inner organic emotional life that you are no longer able to stimulate by any other means. For example, suppose you want to re-create an experience you once had when you were insecure and tentative about expression. If you are successful with the Affective Memory work, it will pique those unconscious insecurities and you will experience similar emotions here and now.

Overall Sensations

This technique involves the whole body, as when you re-create the sensation of being in a shower or lying in the sun. It is often used to practice Sense Memory, but as a choice approach, it can stimulate emotional life for a scene. For example, if you need to be irritable and heat makes you short-tempered, then you would work for heat as an overall sensation. If being covered with sun-tan oil makes you feel sensuous, or if being blown by a cool wind excites and invigorates you, those are the kinds of things that you might choose to work for in other scenes. Here again, you must be sensorially specific, not general.

Animals

A whole book could be written on this approach. Once I spent the better part of a year at the Los Angeles Zoo studying animals and their behavior. As a result I was able to formulate a workable technique for using animals as a choice approach. If you are successful in getting a sense of an animal and can translate it into human behavior, it will affect the way you think, feel, and look! Some of the most exciting work I have ever seen has been the result of a well-executed animal choice. In a class many years ago I was having great difficulty with an earthy character, who was basic, nonintellectual, somewhat animal-like. At last I decided to use a gorilla as a choice. When I began to get a sense of that animal, all the qualities I needed began to emerge as I had never experienced them before. This choice affected my behavior on a multitude of levels and opened doors to me that I didn't even know existed. I have used animals many times since, with similar results. The following lesson provides the details you need to work with animals as a choice approach.

WORKING FOR THE ANIMAL

Using animals as a choice approach involves learning something about rhythm, limitations, tempo, and other aspects of movement.

Rhythm

Study the unique style of movement peculiar to the species of animal that you are working with. For example, there is an elongated, languid rhythm peculiar to the big cats. Squirrels have a short, erratic movement as they dart here and there. Each animal has an overall rhythm that you can identify almost immediately. It is made up of many elements, and in order to accomplish a sense of that rhythm in your own body, you must break the animal's body into sections. I call this technique working with Isolations.

Isolations

If you have ever studied dance you are familiar with certain body Isolations, for you are trained to use parts of your body independently of other parts. The principle is similar when you are working with animals. In order to minimize human limitations of movement, practice Isolations by moving each part of your body as an individual unit separate from the others. Start with your head, moving it from side to side and up and down. As you do this, start moving your shoulders in an up-and-down circular motion. As you accomplish both, start your thorax moving separately from side to side. Attempt to get the sense of your chest and stomach as an entirely separate unit from the rest of your body.

Practice all these Isolations down to the soles of your feet, and do them daily. What this allows you to do is to break the animal down into similar body sections and work with each section at a time. Start with the head . . . watch the animal . . . attempt to get a sense of the rhythm of the head . . . work with it . . . watch the animal . . . go to the shoulders and forget the head . . . watch the animal . . . try to get a sense of the rhythm of the shoulders . . . go to the thorax . . . do the same thing all the way down the body—until you feel you have had some success with each part. Don't worry about the tempo or speed at this point; that will come later. Once you have created all the parts of the animal, slowly put them together. Do the head and shoulders at first, and add other parts until you have the entire rhythm of the animal. Don't be impatient; suddenly it will all come together for you.

Individual Mannerisms

As you work with the animal, you will become aware of mannerisms—the way a cat bends its front paws, for example, or the darting eyes of a small monkey. Study these mannerisms and repeat them through your body until they supplement the rhythms you have already accomplished. As you become more sophisticated in your observations, you will be able to distinguish between species mannerisms and individual mannerisms, because animals are as different from each other as people are.

Corresponding and Contrasting Rhythms

As you learn an animal's rhythms, it is important to identify those that are in contrast to each other and those that complement each other. Take a chicken: Its head moves up and back with a characteristic rhythm, while the rest of the body moves in other rhythms. Study these corresponding and contrasting rhythms. Work with them until you feel a sense of the chicken's movement through your own body.

Having isolated each part of an animal's body, and having worked to get a sense of that area, you should include the rhythm of the area in your concentration of energy. If you "sneak up" on the rhythm of each area, you may be able to hold onto it as you move into another area of the animal's body. It is easier to approach the various rhythms this way, because contrasting rhythms are very difficult to do at first. It is somewhat like rubbing your head and your stomach in circular motions, with each circle going in an opposite direction.

Eric demonstrating how to Work for an Animal at the zoo

When you have worked through the isolation process again and again, you can expect to get a sense of the animal's *overall* movement and rhythm (enamating from the spine), and the *individual* rhythms in each area of the body. If you are specific and don't try to take any short cuts, you will be able to integrate the various rhythms. If you have problems with a particular animal because the contrasting rhythms are so diverse, isolate the different areas and work only with two rhythms until you feel comfortable.

Limitations

As you "build" an animal through your own body, you must include the animal's limitations. Dogs, for example, cannot spread their forelegs to the side. If you have ever tried to do that to a dog, you know how painful it is. Certain monkeys have elongated fingers and a very short thumb and consequently cannot pick up objects the way we do. Most apes have well-developed upper bodies but short, squat hindquarters that make it difficult to walk and run erect. Some animals have such short necks that they have difficulty turning their heads all the way around. As you work with your own animal, you will learn to spot its limitations and include them in your body.

Leading Centers

An animal's leading center is somewhat like the imaginary center that Michael Checkov spoke about in his work. It is the part of the animal's body that leads—the first part to go through a doorway or cross an imaginary line. Find the leading center and then work with it. If, for example, your animal has a leading center at the tip of its nose, allow yourself to be led by the tip of your nose. The same rules apply to humans, too: all people have leading centers!

Secondary Centers

An animal's secondary center closely follows the leading center. If the tip of the nose is the leading center, the lower part of the forelegs might be the secondary center. Work with one center at a time and then put them together.

Years ago, I used a leopard for the lead on a two-part "Kraft Suspense Theatre." The character was a stealthy killer who did his work swiftly and silently; some of the lines in the script said that no one ever heard him as he came and went. I am not an awkard person, but I certainly cannot be described as stealthy or silent. Using the leopard made the difference in my movements and affected my thinking as well. I became aware of everything around me that might be threatening. My reflexes became sharper, and I even felt like a predator. In short, working for the animal along with my other choices helped me to create the character and the emotional realities.

Centers of Weight and Balance

As you observe the animal, look for the center of weight. The bear, for example, carries its weight in the hindquarters, while the gorilla carries it in the upper body. The big cats seem to have theirs evenly distributed, although if you look closely, you will see that they have more weight in the back legs. Get a sense of the animal's weight center and work to exaggerate your own weight in that area of your body until you actually feel heavier there.

Working for the animals' Centers of Weight and Balance

Centers of balance are usually related to weight distribution. The kangaroo, for example is bottom-heavy; consequently its balance is related to that enormous weight in the hindquarters. Notice how an animal handles its balance and decide where the area of balance is.

Centers of Power
Often an animal's center of power is also directly related to the weight center. The gorilla is most powerful in the chest and arms, where its weight is. The kangaroo's greatest power is in the hindquarters, as you know if you have ever seen one leap twenty feet.

Tempo

The complex process of getting an animal's tempo depends largely on developing a sense of all its other areas. Tempo is the speed of movement combined with the unique styles of the animal's movements and behavior: the way it turns its head, for example, or reaches out for an object. Tempo is complex but usually comes as a result of putting all the other elements together.

Having experimented with all the techniques related to getting a sense of an animal, you should now be having some success. You should be creating its rhythms, mannerisms, centers, limitations, and tempo. The sense of the animal should have affected your speech, your thinking, your relations to the people and objects around you.

Now what do you do with what you have accomplished? You certainly can't make an entrance on all fours! Your first line isn't a loud growl. You must *translate* your achievment into human behavior. I have usually approached the translation process by sneaking up on it in small and subtle degrees, progressively becoming more and more human.

Translating the Animal into Human Behavior

Of course, you can simply stand erect in one movement and carry over the animal's rhythms and other behavior to that position. Although I have done this successfully, I recommend that you get to your feet by degrees, first rising to your knees and then inching upward. Do not abruptly take on all your human traits. In the first steps of the translation you should resemble the animal totally, the only difference being that you are standing erect. All other behavior, including the centers and the mannerisms, should be that of the animal.

Naturally you will have to make some adjustment in the animal elements, because your posture is quite different. But remember to retain the sense of the animal in your body at all times. Walk around and explore this sense in the erect position for a while until you get used to the change. Then begin to "subtlize" the various elements, making them more and more human as you go along. You are not eliminating any of the mannerisms or rhythms. You still function in relation to the limitations, but you are humanizing and subtlizing them progressively.

If you do lose the sense of the animal, don't panic. Just assume the animal position again and start exploring the various elements of the process until you regain the feeling of the animal. Then start the translation process again. When you first begin working with animals, the translation bridge is difficult to cross. While you are translating, you will probably have to separate the areas in human form and work with them again, one at a time.

During the translation process feel free to isolate an area and work specifically with it. Or selectively emphasize another area and work primarily with that. Experiment freely! When the time comes that you feel confident with what you have, start improvising around the scene circumstances. If you aren't working on a scene, then relate to the life around you, using the sense of the animal. Take an inventory later to judge how it afffected your behavior.

Experiment with many kinds of animals, making this tool an important part of your craft work. The fun and joy of the world of animals is now open to you, and the possibilities are endless.

Translating the Animal into Human Behavior

SELECTIVE EMPHASIS

Selective emphasis is a craft technique and a choice approach that can be used in a variety of ways: with an available stimulus, with an imaginary stimulus, in a Believability exercise, in imaginary monologues, and with evocative words. It can also be helpful in the choice approach of prior knowledge.

To use selective emphasis, isolate a part or an area of the object. If, for example, you are dealing with an *available stimulus* such as another actor, you might decide to emphasize that person's eyes and relate only to them. This is because his or her eyes make you feel a particular way, and that is the way you want to feel in the scene. You might emphasize a look or a sound in the voice, or you may decide to isolate an odor because it affects you in a certain way. When working with an available stimulus, you can relate to and selectively emphasize any part of the environment—the weather, objects near or far, and so on. The object as a whole may have quite a different effect on you from the part you isolate, and that is why you use selective emphasis.

The technique with an imaginary stimulus is essentially the same except for creating the object. First, work sensorially to build whatever object you want to relate to; and then focus on the specific element of the object that will take you where you want to go. If you are working to endow the other actor with the characteristics of a meaningful person in your life, ask sensory questions comparing and contrasting the actor with the person you have chosen. Then endow the actor with the proper coloring, shape of the mouth and nose, and so on. When you achieve a sense of the person you are working for, you might selectively emphasize, creating pain in his or her eyes or focusing on an emotional quality of some kind. When using selective emphasis, concentrate on the area you have chosen to isolate, but don't cut out all other realities. You must continue to allow yourself to be affected by whatever stin lates responses and to express the life that is going on moment to moment. In the case of select.ve emphasis you may decide to work with just one sense, such as the visual or the auditory, though in other craft work it is wise to use all your senses.

Believability, another powerful tool in itself, can take you almost anywhere when coupled with selective emphasis. The Believability exercise involves mixing a very little truth or a few basic facts into a web of untruths. Two actors in an improvisation may start talking about a particular incident that both of them really experienced. At some point in this discussion, they introduce events that never happened or facts that are untrue. Both actors must go along with the exercise and embellish it as they proceed. For example, suppose that the two had lunch together the day before the rehearsal, and that they had been joined by a friend who happened along. Those are true facts. Now:

He: You know I enjoyed having lunch with you yesterday.

She: I did too.

He: But you needn't have invited Jack to join us as some kind of protector of your virtue!

She: What? I did no such thing. He was just there, and I thought it was only courtesy to ask him to sit down.

He: I really don't believe that; he acted very strangely.

She: You know, I think you're crazy!

He: Ever since we started on this scene, you've been protective and standoffish. Do you think I'm going to attack you?

She: I'm really beginning to get angry, and if you don't stop this interrogation I'm going to leave!

The scene might go on that way until they are quarreling violently.

Selective emphasis is used in Believability practice by creatively leading the exericse in a specific direction. If for example you are obligated to create conflict of some kind, you selectively emphasize Believability behavior that is conflict-oriented.

You can practice Believability alone as well as with another actor. Simply tell *yourself* a story based on truth and weave the untrue Believability elements into it. Again, remember to use selective emphasis to lead yourself creatively in the direction that you want to go. This technique can be employed as a preparation, or it can be used in the body of a scene as a choice.

Selective emphasis is equally effective in combination with Imaginary Monologues. Assume that you are doing a scene with the emotional obligation to feel nostalgic and to reminisce about times gone by. You might choose to talk to someone you really care about who shared those times with you. Such an Imaginary Monologue might run along like this:

> Do you remember when we used to go to football games at school? We bundled up and almost froze to death in the stands . . . What I really enjoyed was going back to the apartment and drinking hot chocolate and listening to music. I loved that time, and I loved the way we were together . . .

The use of selective emphasis with an Imaginary Monologue means that you choose specific elements to talk to the imaginary person about. If nostalgia is the obligation, stay with pleasant experiences and try to avoid thinking or talking about traumatic events.

The *Evocative Words* exercise is best used in relation to selective emphasis. You will recall that Evocative Words as a choice approach consists of saying to yourself words or short phrases connected with a larger experience, in hopes of stimulating the impact of the entire experience. Imagine that you are dealing with an obligation of irritablity. To re-create a certain kind of irritation you might return to a specific experience when you were waiting for your girlfriend and she was very late. For example: "Sitting . . . waiting . . . bench is hard . . . getting cold . . . tired . . . Where is she? . . . She said four o'clock and it's five-thirty . . . This happens all the time . . . tired of it . . . . Sky's getting cloudy . . . I feel stupid sitting here . . . tired . . . bored . . ."

Here again, selective emphasis is used to guide you toward the area where you want to be affected.

Finally, selective emphasis can be compelling in the choice-approach area of *prior knowledge.* As the phrase indicates, this is a situation in which you already have information that can be of professional use to you. The knowledge can be about a person, a place, an episode, or a group of people. If, for example, you have been hired to do a film with an actor who is well established or who is known by some of your colleagues, you may collect quite a bit of prior knowledge about him. Depending on the specific obligations of the scenes you will play with him, you may be able to selectively emphasize some of this information so that it affects you in the way your character in the film should be affected.

For example, imagine that the material obligates you to feel sympathy and respect for the other character and to admire his strength and principles. Perhaps you know that in the past, this actor lost his wife in an accident and that his mother and father died in the same year. Perhaps you also know that you agree with his principles and politics. The knowledge of these things, isolated from the rest of your information about the actor, can stimulate the emotions that you need for the material.

Do not relate to prior knowledge intellectually by simply thinking and reminding yourself of it. Use your senses as part of the process, so that response is organic rather than cerebral. In the case of the actor above, look for the sadness in his eyes, the evidence of stress in the lines of his face, the depth of feeling in his voice, the determination in the set of his mouth and jaw. Make prior knowledge work for you by taking the mental construct and supporting it sensorially.

HOW TO DE-MYSTIFY SCENE WORK

There is so much mysticism related to acting and the language of acting that it is hard to know what an actor is talking about when he discusses his work. What I have discovered is that most actors have only the language; they have not applied it to their work. Yet the only complicated element involved in acting is the human instrument. Since that is truly complex, the bulk of your training should relate to instrumental work. Even a perfectly tuned instrument without a craft, however, is helpless in terms of consistent creativity. In this lesson I want to demystify the technique of creating realities by sketching out a simple blueprint to follow before you start working with a piece of material.

1. Ask yourself what the character is feeling in this scene. (What is the inner organic life?)
2. What has caused him or her to feel this way?
3. Do I understand this emotional life?
4. Have I ever felt like that before? When? What caused it? (If you can, try to identify several experiences that affected you in a similar way.)
5. Break down the elements in each of your personal experiences and translate them into *choices*. For example: You felt somewhat like the character in the scene a month ago, when you sat alone and lonely in your living room waiting for the telephone to ring. The translation depends on creating that place, the objects in the room, the weather, the absence of people, the silent telephone, the sounds and odors related to that time in your life.
6. If you are satisfied with the choice, begin to work sensorially for those elements.
7. Once you have totally explored the choice, you can decide whether or not to use it.

These steps will help you to eliminate the complexity of approaching a scene. Naturally there is other work to be done in fulfilling the scene. If the scene has more than one person, you must deal with the relationship elements, the environment, and several other obligations. However, each obligation can be approached in the same simple manner. Do not complicate! If you are relating to another person, ask yourself how the characters feel about each other and find out what you can do to make yourself feel the same way about the other actor. Confusion is usually the result of not understanding the process. If you understand what to do and how to do it, the confusion disappears. The key question is such a simple one: *What do I want to feel, what would make me feel that, and how can I work toward it?*

HOW TO DIS-OBLIGATE YOURSELF

This "director's" exercise is a two-people involvement, though you can do it very well by yourself. In class I ask one actor to become the "craft director" and help another actor to select the proper preparation for a scene's emotional requirements. The craft director then assists the actor in deciding on an emotional obligation and finding a choice that will stimulate the life desired. Finally, the actor then explores the choice while the craft director makes suggestions and comments on the actor's specific approach. This is a valuable experience for both people. The actor is encouraged to work properly, using his time well and avoiding many of the traps of subjectivity. The craft director, who is personally *dis-obligated* from having to reach an emotional state, can maintain total objectivity.

When the exercise is completed, the actors reverse roles and repeat the process. The actor playing the "craft director" can really see the pitfalls of obligation and subjectivity once the personal obligation to create the reality is removed. An actor who picks up a script knowing that he will be playing the part often blanks out and loses awareness of the ingredients. What he could do easily when he was not involved in the role seems extremely difficult now that there is an obligation to fulfill. By separating yourself, the actor, from your other self, the craft director, you will find it simpler to identify the elements and obligations of the material as well as to select choices and execute them.

This separation has practical value in the early stages of preparation, selection, and working for your choice. But be careful not to continue too far into the process, since the "craft director's" comments may interfere with the impulsive flow. It is simply a matter of knowing when to stop directing yourself.

There are a lot of really good directors out there who don't know when *not* to direct. Don't become one of them!

TAPPING YOUR SUBCONSCIOUS

Much of our real talent originates in the subconscious. When an actor catches fire and begins to function with electrifying creativity, he has made the connection with the subconscious.

Everything that has ever happened to us, every single emotion that we have ever felt, is stored in that part of our psyche. We forget nothing! How do we reach and tap the world of the subconscious? Does it occur purely by accident? Sometimes—and when it does, it usually leaves the actor frustrated and confused.

There are a number of things that you can do, however, to get in constant touch with that "underlife." Though we all tend to suppress painful experiences, and though time clouds and submerges names, dates, and places, you can start keeping a daily journal. Write down your experiences each day, emphasizing the sensory elements of place, people, time, weather—and particularly how you felt. Six months from now, you will look back at the journal and be able to reexperience the things that happened to you. Another technique is the use of Self-Inventory (described in earlier lessons) to take you back to your earliest memories. And here is still another good exercise:

"I'm Five Years Old and I ———"
The actor stands in front of the class, arms at his side. Making eye contact with everyone, he starts with the statement: "I'm Five Years Old and I ———." He fills in the blank with the first impulse that occurs. For example: "I'm Five Years Old and I . . . I'm playin' in the yard . . . I'm five years old and I . . . go to kindergarten, and my teacher is mean and she won't let me play with the clay! I'm five years old and I . . . feel lonely, we move a lot and I always have to make new friends . . ." The actor continues, going up in age from five years to the present. It is important not to think about your responses; the value of the exercise is in being impulsive.

You can do the exercise alone with equally positive results. It is an excellent vulnerability preparation. It opens doors into your memory that have been locked for a long time. It clears the path between the conscious and the unconscious. And of course it suggests choice areas for future exploration.

THE CONCEPTUAL TRAPS OF DIALOGUE

Once for an exercise in my class two actors did a scene from *Same Time Next Year.* The work was wonderful—impulsive, unpredictable, colorful, and filled with surprises. The actors created a relationship that was real and meaningful, full of irreverence, but they took the liberty of paraphrasing the dialogue that the author had written so that they said only about twenty-five percent of the lines verbatim.

In the critique that followed the scene, I told them how much I liked their work and specifically why. The other students agreed that it was really good work. Both actors, however, said that it was much easier to be free and impulsive when they paraphrased the material. As soon as they attempted to speak the author's lines, they began to listen to themselves and silently comment on the results. Then they lost their unpredictability and became self-conscious. I could see that, even though they were delighted with the work they had done, they had not gained the confidence which comes from knowing that you can do it with the lines.

Eric: Okay, you just did some work. Did you enjoy it?

Actors: (in chorus): Oh, yes! Are you kidding? We loved it!

Eric: Right. Well, who did it? You did it—*I* didn't do it! Right?

Actor: Well, yes . . . but . . .

Eric: No buts! The fact is that you are both capable of this kind of work and you just proved it. If you can function at this level of organic reality, then you can do it! So what is it that changes when you attempt to do the lines?

Actress: I don't know; I guess I feel restricted.

Eric: By what?

Actress: By what I think should be in the lines.

Eric: Exactly; by your concept of what each line says. By the logic and meaning of the words. So in effect, you are tailoring your behavior to match the meaning of the words rather than letting the words come from the marvelous impulses that you feel from one moment to the next.

Actor: That sounds great, Eric, but what about fulfilling the scene through the words?

Eric: You do when you allow all that wonderful color and unpredictability to happen! In life our words come directly out of what we feel, and sometimes they seem illogical because of the emotional content. Someone says, ''I hate you,'' to another person, but his voice is filled with love and humor. If you just interpreted the words logically, the emotion would have to be hate . . . right? If you just relate to the words

Eric critiquing a scene

logically and attempt to fufill that concept, you are not only stopping the moment-to-moment life; you are doing something that is unnatural in life. True, we often choose our words when we speak, but for the most part, we express our feelings through the words.

Actor: I understand that, but as soon as I start the lines, something happens and I feel restricted and self-conscious.

Actress: Me too!

Eric: Yes, I understand that. So what can you do about it, besides what you just did? There are a number of ways you can deal with this problem:

One, continue to work for your choices, create the emotional life of the scene, and paraphrase the material, adding more and more of the lines each time you rehearse the scene. That way, you virtually "sneak up" on the words.

Two, be totally *irreverent* about the words. Encourage yourself to express outrageous impulses in the framework of the scene, while saying the author's lines verbatim! This technique allows you to stretch your concepts. Then when you settle back into a more conventional state, you feel less restricted by the concepts.

Three, include the way you feel when you are speaking. If you feel restricted and self-conscious, include those feelings in the lines. Allow your every impulse to color every moment and every word you say.

Four, when you get into trouble, do a Personal Inventory and express everything that it exposes through the words. One of the biggest problems in this area is the dogmatism of the written word! We read the play, we are directed by italics, the director tells us what he wants (usually in result terms: Cry! Laugh! More energy!). Consequently we develop a loyalty to convention and forget our right to contribute! Every time you act, every time you approach a scene, ask yourself this question: *Isn't it possible that the character could behave this way in the scene?* If the author is present, ask him. Most of the time the answer will be, "*Yes,* it is possible that the character could behave in that manner." The author will usually add, "But I hadn't conceived it that way!" Well, don't allow yourself to be chained by the concepts of others. You cannot be truly creative if you allow yourself to be restricted by concept, logic, or someone else's convention.

FULFILLING EMOTIONAL OBLIGATIONS OF MATERIAL

"If you get to a place where you are BEING you, then what? Who wants to see the same character over and over? What about versatility?"

I hear variations of these questions all the time! People are always asking me about the obligation to the author and to the character, and I agree that you *must* fulfill the material on all levels.

The mistake that actors make is to separate themselves from the "character"—to make the character a different person. They think, "I'm not like that, so I have to assume behaviors that *are* like that." When this happens, the game is all over! Everything you do onstage must come from you . . . it must be real and must flow from a real source. If you approach your work with the understanding that all truth lies within you, then the first step is to achieve a here-and-now reality from which to proceed. Once you are BEING, then you can determine the obligations of the "character" and start creating those realities.

Suppose that the character in the play is suspicious, almost paranoid. Throughout the play he furtively glances behind him to see if he is being watched. Well, you know that you're not anything like that; you are secure and trusting by nature. So what do you do? What you *don't* do is assume the character's external behavior. You must understand that you have felt just about every human emotion by the time you are ten years old. You are capable of experiencing any kind of response or physical behavior if you are stimulated by the proper things.

You can start by finding all the things that would make you feel suspicious. Selectively emphasize them—even exaggerate them. Use the available stimuli: the people in the play, the director, the other actors, the technicians, everyone! Look for and *emphasize* anything that makes you imagine or suspect that they don't like you or are talking about you "behind your back." Try to get a sense of being watched from hidden places. Read things into what people say to you. Selectively emphasize all those things, until you feel suspicious and paranoid. Carry your feelings into rehearsal. Before you even realize it, you will be experiencing the same kind of inner life that the character does. The major difference is that now it comes from reality instead of assumption or imposition.

Any character element can be approached in a similar way. *Never* present behavior that has no personal basis. There are many ways to stimulate the behavior that you are obligated to; selective emphasis, the example I use, is only one approach. *What do I want to feel? What might make me feel that way?* You are on the right track! Don't allow yourself to be intimidated and assume behaviors that are not real.

BEING IN EVERY ROLE

The other night I listened to a discussion that a group of people were having about actors. Everyone seemed to agree that some actors are always the same no matter what role they play, and that very few actors are really versatile. The assumption was that the "predictable" actors simply play themselves from one role to another. Then the group began to talk about the marvelous actors who do bring differences into each part. But from my point of view, the actors they all seemed to like are tricky, schticky technicians who do not create reality but wear it.

That group's principal misconception was the notion that the so-called predictable actors are playing themselves. It's just the opposite! An actor who seems to be the same from one part to the next is generally just using things that have worked before. Rather than being in touch with his real impulses, he is encouraging behavior that at one time might have come from an organic source, but now is manufactured. When an actor really functions from organic reality, he is colorful and unpredictable, for he can tap different elements of his personality every time he acts.

Most people think that playing different characters means assuming behaviors and mannerisms, when the truth is that a creative actor stimulates the different "character elements" from his own living fabric. In order to do that every time he acts, he must first get to a place where he is BEING everything he is, expressing everything he feels, and existing comfortably in that state. At this point an actor can introduce a stimulus that will affect the BEING state and cause responses and thoughts that stimulate the kind of behavior the material requires. When this happens, the life onstage is as fresh and new as any reality would be in nature itself. It is impossible to be predictable, since the actor himself does not know what to expect.

Of course, there are a number of variables related to how gifted and talented an actor is to begin with, how inventive he is in the kind of choices he uses in his work, and how well trained he is. His performance may not be as exciting as that of a master craftsman, but if the actor is expressing his moment-to-moment reality, he will not be the same from role to role. Of course he is the same person each time, but that's a plus, not a minus!

CHARACTERIZATION

I'm not sure what most actors mean when they talk about characterization in a play. In fact, I discourage the use of the word "character" in my classes because of the separation between you and the person the playwright describes. It is counterproductive to think of the character as someone different from yourself, particularly if you are doing the role. Naturally there is a character, and just as naturally you must concern yourself with the elements of characterization.

It is necessary, however, to understand the process involved in building a character. The Method is filled with confusing terminology and distorted concepts. I've heard actors say that they *become* the character, that they live the part. It is impossible to be anyone else but you! The idea of becoming anyone else is destructive to the creative process. What should occur as a result of the creative process is that you stimulate thoughts, feelings, and impulses in yourself, from your own frame of reference and your own experiences, that are like the emotional life of the character. By stimulating a point of view as a result of working for choices and being affected, you begin to think, feel, and respond as the person in the play does. In this way you become the character. What actually occurs is that you affect parts of yourself that respond in similar ways.

Many actors spend weeks writing out character background material. They create complex lives for their characters; they invent relatives and relationships that the author never speaks about. They structure the life of the character from birth to the present time—and when they finish this monumental writing task, it usually remains on paper and is never integrated into the actor's work.

Understanding the background and filling in the gaps is important, but the actor's job exists from the point of invention to the point of application. Knowing how, what, where, and why your character does what he does is crucial in looking for choices. It helps you focus on the specific areas in your own life that make you feel what the character feels. But knowing what to do from the point of understanding the character, and then doing it, is the place where most actors fall down. Ask yourself these questions next time you approach a part:

> What does the character feel?
> Why does he feel that way?
> What are the realities that have gone into making this person the way he is?

Then ask:

> What would make me feel that way?
> What in my life experience can I use that would stimulate those things in me?

Begin to explore those choices sensorially until you get the responses you desire.

NOTES

NOTES

NOTES

NOTES

NOTES

NOTES

THE BUSINESS

THE BUSINESS

Often a theoretical way of working sounds good and succeeds in a laboratory situation, but fails to be usable when put to the commercial test. This section attempts to deal with that very important bridge between the workshop and the sound stage, between your living room and the casting office. It covers what to do and how to do it when you are faced with the pressure of getting the job and performing the part. I have attempted to separate the realities from the fantasies and, I hope, have shown how to maintain your integrity in a business that threatens personal integrity.

As most of you know, there is usually a great deal of difference between rehearsals and opening night. It is when the director says ''Action!'' that the actor needs a strong craft and technique and the ability to use all his years of training. If at the ''moment of truth'' your work fails you, then you cannot count on it as a professional approach. This section shows how to triumph during those difficult moments by using an approach that you *can* count on.

THE IMPORTANCE OF A WORKSHOP

The ability to explore and experiment is essential to acting. The artist must have a place to *fail*. You can't do it out there in filmland, so you must have a laboratory where you can take chances and expose yourself on a level that won't hurt you in the business.

There are a number of good classes in most big towns. If you ask around, you can get recommendations. Then visit several classes and judge for yourself; you will be allowed to audit most of them at least once. Choose the work and the teacher that most pique your interest and challenge your instrument. A good way to find the right workshop is to call the Screen Actors Guild or Actors Equity, or go to an actor whose work you admire and inquire about his training. Don't be taken in by high-sounding advertisements.

There are also a number of workshops that cater to the professional actor who has already been trained. These are good supplements to a regular class. Wherever you decide to go, it is important to practice your instrumental work and use your craft daily. You cannot work in a vacuum, so you must receive qualified criticism. If you cannot explore your impulses and experience the moment-to-moment emotions that are going on inside, then you will never really know what your emotional perimeters are, nor will you be able to grow as an artist. The laboratory or workshop is a place that affords you this opportunity.

COMMITMENT TO ACTING

I have been in Hollywood for a number of years, and a lot of the people I used to see are no longer around. What happened to them? I often wonder about this sea of nameless faces that professed undying commitment to their art and their work. Everybody knows it's a tough business, and the casualty rate is very high. We all accept the fact that there is enormous competition and not enough work to go around. We are aware that there are no guarantees, only hopes. Actors come to my classes, seemingly filled with fire and energy, exclaiming about their love for acting, and leave like a wisp of smoke without reason or trace.

What causes the disappearance of so many actors who seemed to be sincere about their commitment? I'm sure there are a variety of reasons—economic, domestic, and many others—but I believe that the critical factor behind the decisions to stay or go is love for acting. It takes great passion to sustain the disappointments and hardships dealt out in this field.

Many times I have heard actors say, "I don't want to be a star; I just want to work a lot!" *Everybody* wants to be a star, and there's nothing wrong with that. But beneath these desires, hopes, and dreams, one has to have a true love for the work. I think that this is the quality responsible for success. I'm not just referring to financial success, but to the most important kind of success there is: doing what you want to do with your life, and being happy about it. We all need recognition and appreciation, and it's nice to hear that our work is good and that it moved someone. That's the cherry on the cake—but it won't keep you committed.

It is the discovery of the art and the process that will start your love affair with acting. It is the excitement of experiencing an emotional life resulting from your choices. This kind of commitment is not a sometime thing. It comes from the discipline that you acquire by working at your craft every day of your life. And every time you are knocked down by failure, frustration, and criticism, *you must be able to bounce back up* and continue to work. It is the actors like this that I still see around. Some of them are very successful in the industry; all of them are successful as people.

I hope I have not given the impression that craft and instrumental work are filled with agonizing problems and frustrations. The greatest enjoyment of your life will come when you can function from your own BEING foundation. If you do the work and learn to use your instrument organically, you will experience "highs" you never dreamed possible. When an older person asks me if it is too late to start acting, or too late to go back to it, I always say that it is never too late to create something! It is never too late to make yourself happy! The purpose of this book is to share exercises and techniques that will help you maintain your dedication to a life of creativity and excitement.

THE TRUTH ABOUT THE BUSINESS

A real problem that actors face is justifying the time spent training when endless periods pass without work. Most actors come to this crossroads more than once, and it is then that many leave their acting classes and stop working on their instrument and craft. Soon they aren't doing anything productive; their attitude is, "What's it all for, anyway? I'm not working, so why break my back studying year after year?" Among the many reasons for the breakdown of belief, a major one is the lack of commercial reward and recognition.

The fact is that theatres, movies, television are businesses run to make money! The people running them are not interested in art or beauty, but in box office grosses, costs, distribution, exhibitors, and return on investment. When they cast a production their concern is, Does this actor or that actress pull crowds at the box office? If you are new to the business, most of the casting people are afraid to take the chance that you might give them trouble on the set because of your inexperience. Trouble costs time, and time means money. So their tendency is to go with the tried and true.

These are the facts that you must know and accept. There are, of course, exceptions—people who will take chances on new talent because they are interested in more than the money. But they are in the minority, whereas the majority keep lists of preferred actors and actresses. These listed performers are the ones who work the most, particularly in television. The competition is fierce, there are literally hundreds of actors for every role cast, and that's the way it is.

If you are willing to accept the *realities* of the field you have chosen, you will be far ahead of the actor who lives on fantasy. If you know the odds and face them honestly, it will be much easier to do what you must do. An actor *must* find the joy and fulfillment of working on the craft an end in itself. You don't become a better actor just so that you can work in television; you do it for yourself, because you love to act and the creative process turns you on.

What makes you an artist is the fulfillment that comes from falling in love with the process. Naturally you want to work and earn a living at your art, and that is as it should be. If you are talented, if you develop that talent, if you commit yourself to a life of growth, and if you have the will and tenacity to stick in there, you will ultimately succeed. One of the great tragedies of history is that the artist Vincent Van Gogh sold only one painting in his life. But his love for his art and his passionate commitment to it must have given him something that most people don't even know exists.

TAKING RESPONSIBILITY

When you are asked, "What do you do?" and respond, "I'm an actor," how many times are you met with a complex "Oh . . ." and a short silence? If you had said you were a doctor, lawyer, or any other "respectable" professional, the person inquiring would have been properly impressed. Why don't people give the same respect to actors? It takes as many, or in some cases more, years to become a fine actor as it does to become qualified in other professions. As a matter of fact, acting is one of the most unsure professions. If you go into engineering or accounting, at the end of your training and apprenticeship you have some assurance of employment. Committing your life to acting takes enormous courage, desire, and awareness of the hardships ahead. Why is it, then, that unless you are an obvious success, people do not honor you for being an actor?

There are a number of reasons for their lack of respect. In many countries over the centuries actors have been outlawed and considered criminals and "cutpurses." Stigmas of immorality and irresponsibility have been attached to them. Today we are looked on as lazy do-nothings who live on unemployment benefits and hang out with others of our kind, all of us waiting for a telephone call that doesn't come.

I think *we* are responsible for that image! We support it in many ways. All a person has to do to be an "actor" in our society is to step off a bus from anywhere and say "I am an actor." That person can get a set of pictures, hunt for an agent, compete for employment, and in some cases get a job here and there. Please don't misunderstand me. I'm not trying to change the system or curtail the freedom of the individual. What I do challenge is our attitude toward our profession, our commitment to it, and above all, the preparation involved. You can't change the world, but you can change the way you relate to it. If more actors would become involved in the seriousness of the preparation, of getting ready to do what they must do in order to act, there would be a new feeling among us that would carry over into the world. We could relate to our profession with nobility and pride because we would feel we had earned the right to it.

If you worked every day at your craft and could feel your growth, if you knew that you had a craft which was a result of years of labor and love, then you would walk tall. Producers and directors often show little respect for us, and again, it's our fault! If you know what you are, what you are doing, and *how* to do it, no one can abuse you! Self-assurance comes from confidence, and confidence can only come from hard work and training. If you get up each morning and spend a good part of the day doing your work, you will begin to feel special about yourself. When you stand in front of the camera, you will no longer quake with fear and tension and hope just to get through it.

The work I refer to is an ongoing process that never ends. As George Bernard Shaw once said: ''Success is ten percent inspiration and ninety percent perspiration.'' You must work, work, work, and when you are fatigued, work some more. Here's a good prescription:

1. Find a good class and focus on your training.
2. Do your homework every day.
3. Keep your peace of mind by fulfilling your financial responsibilities.
4. Do a lot of scene work.
5. Take and use all productive criticism.
6. Work in the theatre whenever possible.
7. Jump at every opportunity to act.

Remember that you are one of a kind! Develop your own individuality.

DEALING WITH INACTIVITY AND DEPRESSION

Most actors are familiar with depression. Even those who are well established have to face the feast-and-famine realities of the business.

How often do you get depressed about not working? It is difficult not to feel personally rejected when no one seems to want you. Time appears to drag endlessly and you have to invent things to fill it with. You go where other actors congregate so you can share your boredom and inactivity. The talk is usually about the business or about acting or about who's doing what where. After several hours and four million cups of coffee, you amble home and stare expectantly at your telephone. You call your service and find that you have no messages. You read the trades . . . watch a little television . . . calculate when your unemployment check is due. Finally you take a nap, not because you feel tired but because you don't want to face the creeping depression that comes with nightfall. This goes on day after day, until the weeks stretch into months and years.

Is that any way to live? Of course it isn't; there is no reason to face such a routine. Don't feel immune to these traps, however. They can sneak up on you until before you know it, you're involved in some kind of life-wasting inactivity.

WHAT CAN YOU DO TO HELP YOURSELF?

First you must understand the realities of the profession you have chosen.

Deal with the economics of living. Get a job and fulfill your financial obligations. That sounds mundane, but it adds to your self-respect.

Exercise your body: take care of the physical instrument!

Work on your instrument and craft four or five hours every day.

Diversify your creative energy: paint, write, stage-manage, direct. Even if you can't perform them on a professional level, these activities keep you productive and therefore minimize depression.

Get into a class, a play, or both!

Fill your life with active and productive people—people who are doing things.

Keep a journal; write down your activities and thoughts so you can relate to them at another time.

Set goals for yourself that you can accomplish daily.

Involve yourself in a variety of stimulating activities. Acting may be the most important thing in your life, but it isn't the only valuable project in the world.

Read! Read! Understand your field and the people who have made important discoveries and contributions.

Read all the acting books; read every play you can get hold of. Also see plays and films; know what is happening in your field!

USING YOUR TIME PRODUCTIVELY

"Oh, Eric, I'm so tired of the hassle!" Sensitive and talented actors have told me this. "I'm sick of waiting for the phone to ring. I hate going on interviews and being treated like a piece of meat. I'm bored, tired, and lonely, and I don't think I can take much more!" "Do you want to act?" I ask. "Of course I do, but I can't deal with the other stuff." they reply.

The casualty rate in this business is enormous. People come to town every day and go the picture, agent, interview route. They hang in there for a time in spite of the distress and pain; then they get discouraged and go home. What do you do about the realities that exist in this business? How can you deal with the hurt and the rejection and the insensitivity that you are faced with daily? It's not easy!

First of all, you must be aware of the hard facts. Then you need to know whether being an actor is something you *must* do. Is it what you want to commit your life to, or is it a fling that you want for a couple of years?

Are you prepared for the years of training ahead of you? You must learn your craft so that you can deliver when you get your shot. You must fill your time with productive activity so that the waiting does not destroy you. You must deal with the economic realities of supporting yourself while you pursue your career. Above all, you must use your time productively.

Set aside a period every day to work on your craft. Split your time between instrumental work and craft techniques. Know exactly what you are going to do each day, so you won't just sit there and waste the time. As you grow you will become familiar with your obstacles and know how to deal with them. Below is a suggested list of daily work that has been described in detail earlier in the book.

Relaxation
Do the various relaxation exercises to learn how to use them, even though you probably won't be tense at home alone.

Sensitize
Practice this exercise every day—more than once, if you can.

Personal Inventory
Taking Personal Inventory several times a day is at the heart of your instrumental development.

Sense Memory
Sense Memory exercises are a bridge between instrumental and craft work.

Ego Exercises
Instrumental preparation through ego exercises helps to keep your sense of self intact.

Observation Exercises
Watching people everywhere you go is essential for your growth as an actor.

Animal Work
Spend time at the zoo working on getting a sense of animals.

Choice Exploration
Approach choices for preparing a scene through taking Self-Inventory, cataloging choices, identifying the choice you want, and exploring its application.

OUTER OFFICE, INNER OFFICE

Actor: Okay, I'm learning what to do once I get the job, but how do I get it in the first place?

Eric: You mean on the interview?

Actor: Yes, how do I behave? What can I do that will put me in a favorable light?

Eric: BE who you are!

Actor: What do you mean BE who I am?

Eric: Just that. Don't do any more or less than what you feel. Express what you do feel and get involved with the people who are interviewing you.

Actor: I'm usually very tense on an interview, and I can't let them see that!

Eric: Well, first off, deal with your tension and alleviate it as best you can. Then you should allow what is left to be seen, while focusing your attention outward.

At this I usually get a glassy-eyed stare, because the actor doesn't accept it. Most people think that if they find the formula for behavior on interviews, they will generally get the job. Not true! There isn't any formula . . . there aren't any tried and true ways to ensure success. You really don't know what "they" have in mind, you don't know what their concepts are, and you can't mind-read or second-guess other people. The only thing you have to sell is yourself, and most actors bury their own treasure by being affable and social and "talking the talk." When you have had your interview and are driving home, you can look back on the whole thing and realize that no one ever saw *you!*

Actor: All right, enough preaching about BEING! Give me something concrete that I can use.

THE OUTER OFFICE

This is the place where most actors sit and "out-cool" each other. They behave as if this were the thirty-third interview of their day and they have to be on the set to shoot at two o'clock. They put out a lot of inane small talk and untrue stories about what they are being considered for. A *total* waste of time!

This is the moment to deal with your tension, do some relaxation exercises, ask yourself (semiaudibly) how you feel, and express moment-to-moment realities. Continue to expose all your demons until you are completely in touch with how you feel, and until you are expressing it. Once you become less tense and begin functioning in terms of what really is going on, try to get involved in observing and perceiving the other people in the room. Involvement helps to get you away from your problems and takes you off the "spot."

Next, find out from the secretary if there is any material you can look at. If there is, read it for content and try to understand the entire piece. Look at the part that you will be considered for and think about the emotional life of the character. *Don't act! Don't make any decisions* about how you are going to read it! Just familiarize yourself with the words and try to get some understanding of what is going on. If you start to assume behaviors or "get into it," you might find that the interviewers want something entirely different.

THE INNER OFFICE

Here two, three, or more people, dressed in business suits or "early Palm Springs" tennis clothes, are sitting and oozing charm, expressing interest in you that they usually don't feel. One of them may say "Hi, how are you? Sit down make yourself comfortable . . . What have you done recently?" At this point the actor usually suppresses everything he really feels and becomes even more charming than they are, hiding the enormity of his need. A little voice inside him keeps repeating, "Oh please, let them like me . . . I really need this part!"

The small talk goes on for a minute or two, and then they tell you a bit about what they want and ask you to read. If you have any questions, you usually make them brief so as not to be a nuisance. You don't really hear what they say, because you are too tense to listen. You do the best you can to assume attitudes and behaviors that might hit some of the emotions they are after. Of course, even if you do indicate some of the emotional life they are looking for, it will not stem from an organic source. Another total waste of time!

Instead of carrying on the inner-office charade, let them see how you really feel. If you are anxious, let it show! "Hi, how are you?" "Hi . . . I feel a little anxious . . . I really would like to get this part." Such a surprising change might throw them momentarily, but forge ahead and BE who you are! Tell the truth, and ask as many questions as you need to.

Once you understand what they are looking for, ask for a couple of minutes. Start working for choices that will make you feel what the character feels at that time. Try to use all available realities. Include all the emotional impulses that you are experiencing. BE, every moment you are there, and allow yourself to come through in that reading. If you don't like what you just did, ask them if you can read again. TAKE YOUR SPACE.

COLD READING

Time is the most valuable thing in life, yet we all fall into traps that waste time. If you are not working at a regular job and don't have a specific routine, you find that you spend a lot of time waiting for "something to happen." There are a lot of ways that we waste time, thinking we are doing something creative when actually we are not.

Too many actors think they are working on their craft by practicing cold reading, or doing vocal work to improve their voice so that they can become better cold readers. "You have to be able to read cold in order to get the job in the first place," they say. Of course you have to get the job in order to use your craft, but I am not convinced that impositional, result-oriented learning techniques are the way to go about it. There are classes that teach cold reading, and other classes that teach you how to behave in an interview; but in my opinion your time could be used better in learning to BE who you are.

I think that most involvements with cold reading are anticreative. If you can simply read aloud, then you can deal with the technical elements of reading a piece of material. But if you learn how to deliver emotion technically while reading, you are in effect assuming behavior that does not come from an organic source. A lot of potentially good actors become facile fakers, and these reading techniques carry over into performance. Pretty soon the actors have difficulty distinguishing between what they really feel and what they deliver as the desired behavior. "Instant acting" is not a creative solution. But if you know what to do and how to do it, you can not only get the job but get it without violating reality.

I've been an actor for thirty-one years, and in all that time, no one ever shoved a script into my hand and told me to read. I could always have five or ten minutes to look it over. In that five or ten minutes, you can do your work.

First: Read the material through a couple of times just to become familiar with the syntax. Get an idea of the style of the piece and the placement of all the periods and commas. *Do not* make any decisions about the emotional obligations at this point!

Second: When you feel comfortable with the words, read it again and try to determine what is happening between the people. What is your character doing and feeling? How is he or she relating to the other characters?

Third: Get an understanding of the emotional obligations. For example, the character you are reading for is distraught over the death of his wife and can hardly speak without breaking down. Now you know what he is feeling and why.

Fourth: This is the point at which you must use most of your craft ability and knowledge. *Do not* assume an attitude or behavior of any kind. Instead, do some Personal Inventory. Find out how you feel here and now, encourage the expression of your moment-to-moment life, and then ask yourself what would make you feel the way the character does. Make a choice that's within your reach, and begin to work for it. You might sensorially try to create the death of someone whom you love. If you are successful with your choice work, you can be confident that when you read, it will be real, compelling, and unpredictable. The life that results from such a process is much more exciting than most of the "cold readings" that are technically delivered.

AN ACTOR MUST ACT

"Dad, Mother, I've decided to be an actor!" There is a long silence. Finally your parents begin to ask questions about the stability and dependability of such a choice. You tell them that it's the only thing that excites you and that you love it and must follow that course. After a few more attempts to convince you of the hazards, your parents, who love you and want you to be happy, reluctantly encourage you to pursue your dreams. You go to school or to a workshop, you do scenes and plays, and when you think you're ready, you put yourself on the market.

That's when the wait begins. The struggle grips you, and reality starts to corrode your enthusiasm. It becomes clear that you are totally dependent on others for employment. At first you keep your hope and excitement alive by a variety of rationalizations, but soon you must deal with the depression of interminable periods of inactivity. The casualty rate is enormous. "Whatever happened to Joe?" "Oh, he went back home."

But it need not turn out that way. If you truly love to act, then act! Create your own opportunities; find material that excites you and do it. Get into a play; and if that is impossible, gather a bunch of your actor friends, find a director, and put on your own play. If you can't afford to rent a theatre, perform it in hospitals, children's homes, and correctional institutions. Find a piece of material and do a one-man or -woman show. Volunteer your services to the city, state, or federal government. ACT! ACT! ACT!

The real problem is that most people pursue this career for the wrong reasons. We all grew up with the movies, admired certain movie heroes, and yearned to be like them. The magic of stardom, the Cinderella glamour, anesthetizes us. Acting becomes a means to that end instead of the end in itself. If that is the basis of your motivation, the harsh realities soon taint your desires. But if you love to act and feel fulfilled by the process of creating life on the stage, no one can stop you.

''The part's too small.'' ''I can't do that—it will hurt my career.'' ''I haven't worked all these years just so that I can do a small scene.'' Those are the ego-based excuses you give yourself for not doing what you love to do. Last year in London I walked through the theatre district and saw the names and pictures of well-established English actors in small parts. They act constantly, sometimes in the lead, sometimes in small roles. We expend so much worry on what other people think, instead of doing what we love. Get up in the morning and go to the library; find something that appeals to you; start working on it, and when you feel ready, invite a group of your friends to your home and do it for them! If you like the piece, take it someplace else. Do a staged reading, or write something yourself. But stop waiting for others to give you the opportunity to do what you love to do. It's your life. Take the helm and follow your own course!

TALENT

Have you ever wondered what *talent* is? There's a lot of talk about acting talent—who has it and who hasn't. Is it a rare gift born only to a few? Is it something that infects you in grade school? Is it something you inherit, or is it acquired during maturation? Do you have it? You must have some, because everyone liked you in the school play! But is it real? Is it enough? What the hell is talent?

I have heard many descriptions of talent: "It's sensitivity!" "It's feeling!" "It's imagination!" "It's theatricality!" "It's the ability to view life a certain way!" To have talent, I think you must have all these qualities and more. At the same time, I don't think talent is rare or mystical at all. I believe that the talent for acting is quite common, and that with training almost anyone can be taught to act. Think about all those young actors who are awful when they first begin to appear in films, yet over the years develop into competent actors. Did they develop talent, or did they have talent to begin with? Naturally there are varying degrees of ability, and some actors can do better work than others. I believe that talent isn't rare, but the development of it is very rare. The training and years of arduous work are uncommon among actors. Most actors say: "I don't go to classes; it's a bunch of bull! If you can act, you act." Or "I don't want to interfere with my talent by congesting it with a lot of intellectual nonsense! I'm not going to be a classroom actor!" You've all heard those comments. They are like saying, "I'm going to be an astronaut, but I'm not going to waste time learning to fly or studying the theories of flight." Good luck!

Here is my loose definition of talent: the ability to perceive and be affected by an enormous number of stimuli, and to be able to express those feelings, responses, and impulses imaginatively and colorfully. I would say that this is a basic description of the superstructure of talent for acting. How many affectable and expressive people do you know who are not actors? I'm sure there are quite a number. Could these people be taught to act? Of course they could! In addition to people who are already expressive, there is an army of inhibited and suppressed people who could be trained to act very well. What they need is to remove the obstacles and eliminate the problems that cause the inhibitions.

So what am I saying? Make actors out of everyone? Corner the mailman and seduce him into a career in the theatre? Woo the meat cutter away from Ralph's Supermarket and put him in films? No, No. We don't need more competition than we already have! The point is that training and commitment to work are the major ingredients in the development of your talent, and that you cannot lie around while your natural gifts win out. The world is full of people who have lived on the fantasy of success for years, only to end up walking down some lonely street and muttering to themselves.

Do the exercises I've told you about. Do them every day! Get into a good acting class with a teacher whom you relate to, and work on your craft! Do scene work every week. Confront your problems and eliminate them. Grow—and demand more and more of yourself. Eventually you will be able to see and understand your own growth. More important, you will know *how* to do what you have to do when you act, and no one will ever be able to take that away from you. At this point the mystique will no longer exist, and you won't have to live on hope alone.

NURTURING THE EGO STATE

When things are going well you feel good about yourself, but an actor's ego state has a tendency to fluctuate. Businessmen work regularly, and doctors and lawyers constantly see clients. But actors usually spend a great deal of time between jobs, and that inactivity has a brutal effect on the ego. When you feel unproductive, useless, and without direction, don't sweep your mood under the carpet. It is better to acknowledge that your depressions exist, because then you can do something about them.

Actors suffer from a variety of ego ailments, insidious demons that whisper to them, "You're not good enough . . . Nobody wants you . . . You're too old . . . You're too young . . . You're not good-looking enough . . . You don't have enough talent . . . Who are you to think you can do it? . . . You never went to college . . . You're a fool to keep trying." In my classes the actor's ego state becomes a part of his overall preparation. Specifically, the actor's instrumental work includes ego preparations.

The first step is to find out how you feel about yourself, both generally and in a variety of situations. You must level with yourself and be totally honest about what you discover! Of course, the ego state will be in greater jeopardy when there is something at stake—when you are working professionally, for example.

It is important that you do not base your sense of ego or well-being on your work alone. You are a human being first, and you have value above and beyond your work. Each day remind yourself that you are who you are, and that you have value and important qualities as an individual apart from acting. That knowledge will not depreciate your commitment or love for your art. On the contrary, it will allow you to put it into proper perspective.

Ego Perspective

Do this exercise every morning the same way you do Personal Inventory. Ask questions of yourself: "Who am I? . . . What do I want? . . . What can I do? . . . How do I feel about the people in my life? . . . How do they feel about me? . . . What have I accomplished as a person? . . . What have I been able to do for others? . . . If there were no such thing as acting, what value would I have? . . . What other talents do I have? . . . How do I feel about the world? . . . What are the good things that people have said to me or about me?"

If you practice the Ego Perspective exercise every day, it will help you to separate yourself from your dependencies on your work. It will give you perspective on yourself as an entity, apart from your role in a fickle industry. The state of the ego can make the difference between functioning and not functioning.

CONSISTENT HARD WORK

In the film *The Turning Point,* which deals with ballet, all the dancers take hours and hours of classes every day. The stars do their bar work and exercise side-by-side with the new members of the company.

How many actors, including yourself, do you know who work on their instrument and craft every day? Not many, I'll bet! Why is that? First, a lot of people act for the wrong reasons; they come to Hollywood to fulfill their childhood fantasy of becoming a "movie star." The movies of the forties, fifties, and even the early sixties were full of stories about novices hitting it big in Hollywood. Although that has happened, it is definitely an exception!

Second, most actors don't know what to do in order to work at their craft. There are not a lot of places where the actor can receive good training, and even if there were, not many actors feel the need for it. A prepared actor, by my definition, knows his instrument intimately, can identify his personal obstacles to creating, and has complete mastery of a craft that allows him to eliminate the blocks and originate exciting reality on the stage or in front of the camera. That ability takes years of commitment and work. It takes a love for the process and a belief in the results of that process.

My students say "Years of work? That's depressing, Eric!" I always point out that those years will pass anyway. How much further ahead you will be if you use them to grow!

Amber Facing Reality about her acting career

FACING REALITY

If you ask any person in the world what he or she wants most, I think the honest answer would be happiness! Of course, the key to happiness varies with each person, but it often involves doing the kind of work that you like. For the actor, however, the opportunity to be gainfully employed in acting is less available than in most other fields. So how do you maintain your happiness with so little work? That is a question that far too many actors never considered when they entered the field, much to their dismay later on.

The entire BEING concept is built on reality! It means living in terms of truth, adjusting your life to what really exists. If you have chosen to act, and if that is what you must do, then start to explore the realities. Know what you are dealing with, and make your living adjustments accordingly.

Reality: It is an overcrowded field filled with incredible competition.
Actor: I know that. I accept that! I am prepared to face the competition and the rejection.
Reality: There aren't any guarantees.
Actor: I realize that, and I'm willing to do my work and take my chances.
Reality: You may go for months and even years without work.
Actor: I hope that isn't the case. But I'm prepared for it, and in the interim I will spend my time working on being a better actor.
Reality: You must eat and pay your bills in the meantime.
Actor: I understand that I must fulfill my responsibilities. I'll do so by working in other areas—enjoyable ones, I hope.
Reality: Even when you do work, at times you will be faced with insensitive direction and an atmosphere that makes creativity almost impossible.
Actor: I know that. My only defense is to know my instrument and craft so thoroughly that I will be able to do good work in spite of the difficulties.
Reality: The ego suffers tremendously as a result of waiting and wanting.
Actor: I'm not Superman, and I know I'll get discouraged. But I will do my best to keep things in perspective and keep my ego healthy.
Reality: There are a thousand other things you could do for a living that offer more security, more money, and probably more recognition.
Actor: I know that too. It isn't a matter of making a simple choice between this or that; acting is what I must do, and I intend to do it for *me*.
Reality: The preparation for acting and the actual work itself are both very hard. Contrary to what people may think, acting is hard, hard, work!
Actor: Yes, it's a twenty-four-hour-a-day involvement—a labor of love! For me, it's harder *not* to act.

Reality: There are other people involved in your life, and they may have to make many sacrifices for your commitment.

Actor: That's a point, all right. And an intelligent person has to weigh value over value and decide what he must do. Frederick S. Perls wrote, "I do my thing, and you do your thing. I am not in this world to live up to your expectations, and you are not in this world to live up to mine. You are you, and I am I, and if by chance we find each other, it's beautiful."

There are thousands of other realities, and it is easy to avoid facing them; but they will sneak up on you in the night! Acknowledge the truth of things as they present themselves. Don't sweep them under the rug, and you will be able to make positive adjustments all along the way.

MAINTAINING YOUR PERSONAL INTEGRITY

It is easy to maintain your integrity when you have a full stomach. The test is to honor your principles and hang onto your integrity when you're hungry and desperate to work. The first step is to know who you are and what you want. Commit yourself to a way of work and train yourself to be the best craftsman that you can. Come to terms with your worth, and trust that you have value as a person and an artist. When you get an opportunity to work in a film or play, make sure that the viewpoint of the material and the production does not violate your beliefs. Of course differences in interpretations can be discussed and arbitrated, but don't take work that compromises your deep convictions. Never do "crap" for the money: don't play a character that glorifies something you abhor, or give up your own level of reality in the work process, or abandon your creative contribution out of fear that you might be replaced. God knows that it's hard to get work, but every time that you compromise your principles and surrender your integrity, you give up something that erodes your power, individuality, and ability to respect yourself. When those elements leave you, a chain reaction of "settling" begins, and your work becomes commonplace and predictable. The whip that is often used on the actor is that he is "temperamental" and "hard to work with." He can find himself on "lists" that keep him from working and put him out of business. Nevertheless, if you can substantiate your beliefs and principles, that's not temperament!

We exist in a business where most people are "running scared." It is often difficult to maintain your values, but maintain them you must. In the play *The Velvet Trap,* the character, a Hollywood screenwriter, says, "They give you a thousand a week until you need a thousand a week, and that's when they own you." How many times have I heard actors say "Well, you have to earn a living!" I say, "If it means giving up your soul, drive a taxi!" The irony is that if you keep your integrity, if you hold onto your principles, if you develop your true talent and unique point of view, you will leave this earth having made a contribution that will outlast the work of all the "copouts."

You may be thinking that it's easy to say all these noble things but not easy to do them. You're right!

IRREVERENT ACTING

Traditionally the actor has been considered a re-creative artist, while the writer and director have enjoyed the reputations of creators. The writer creates the plot, draws the characters and their relationships, and describes how they think and behave. The director supplies his statement. Meanwhile the actor is expected to mouth the author's words, follow the director's suggestions, and be moved like a "re-creative puppet" from one scene to the next.

That's not how it should be, I believe. The actor, the third part of that creative triumvirate, brings to a play the same amount of original creative reality as the playwright and the director. The actor must stimulate dimension and bring elements of expression and impulsive life to the character that the author may never have conceived of. To this end the actor must have the space to be "irreverent" toward the material for a period of time during rehearsal. He must be allowed, and must allow himself, to go wherever his choices take him, even if they seem to stray from the author's concept of the character.

The kind of excitement that an actor can bring to a role is his creative contribution, which is equal to the contribution of the author and the director. If fear and intimidation get in the way of the actor's craft, and he allows his insecurities to stop him from doing his work, he will surely remain a puppet.

On a moment-to-moment level, the actor experiences impulses that lead to other impulses. He affects the other actors and in turn is affected by their responses. This kind of life leads to surprises, unpredictability, and good ensemble work.

There are a number of techniques and exercises that help you train yourself to trust your impulses. First you must accept the right to be what you are and express what you feel, even if it is ''irreverent'' to someone else's concepts. When you are totally willing to follow your feelings wherever they take you, more often than not the life that evolves not only serves the material but creates a fullness of character that goes beyond the author's original concept of the play and the characters.

During the rehearsal period you should use all your time productively. Explore and experiment with choices, ventilate all your impulses, try a variety of choice approaches, and be courageous in your expression! Although the greatest amount of irreverence should take place during the rehearsal period, irreverence is not limited to rehearsal. It is a freedom the actor must grant himself if he is to allow the organic impulses to flow. When you know what the emotional obligations are, when you have some concept of the behavior you are after, when you have been told by the author (in italics) what you should be projecting, and when the director has influenced your thinking, it is very difficult not to obligate yourself to ''result'' work. But what you must do is work for the specific choice you have decided on and express the moment-to-moment life that is happening.

Express your impulses through the dialogue, continue to work for the choice, and allow whatever you feel to come out in the scene, no matter how irreverent it might be. As a matter of fact, you can even encourage expression of the outrageous impulses that you feel. Several things occur when you approach material in this manner: First, you stimulate an organic level of reality that flows from one moment into the next, clearing your instrument of blocks and suppression. Secondly, you are in a position to discover a variety of life that might add color and dimension to what the author wrote. Thirdly, you are creatively using your instrument in the way that it was meant to be used.

If your irreverence leads you astray and you are really misinterpreting the piece, then make other choices. However, continue to allow whatever you feel to be exposed, no matter how irreverent. It takes guts and courage to do this kind of work, and it also takes the training to know how to do it. An actor who chooses to be irreverent without the proper instrumental and craft training is being not irreverent but irresponsible! The right to your creative freedom does not carry with it the license to distort another person's creation. The aim is to fulfill the material and add further dimension that comes from your creative process. All this is indeed possible if you are true to yourself and the craft you have worked to learn.

LEVELING

Once when I was a guest on an interview show for television, I could feel the demon of tension crawling around my body just before we taped. I had to wait to go on, and that made it worse. I acknowledged it and expressed it to myself and attempted to get involved with the people there. All my exercise work helped, and I was better off by the time we started to tape. Because of the nature of the show, I had the freedom to express how I felt, and I admitted my discomfort. I talked about the obligation of behaving like a guest on a talk show and how I didn't want to fall into the trap of that image. The host responded well to what I exposed and we were off on a solid level of reality. I continued to express my true feelings throughout the interview, and so did he.

At the moment of truth, when the director says ''Action'' or when you get the five-second signal, the heart starts to beat more rapidly, the mouth gets dry, the palms of your hands grow moist, and you are at the crossroads. One road leads to covering it up and functioning in spite of your discomfort, and the other road points to dealing with it. Naturally if you are doing a dramatic show, you don't have the freedom that I had in the television interview. You can't turn to the camera in the middle of the scene and talk about how tense you are. However, you can expose it by including your moment-to-moment impulses in the framework of the lines. That frees you of the tension by expressing it through the dialogue. It also gives the character more dimension and unpredictability. I realize that what I'm suggesting takes courage and does involve some risk. Whenever you violate conventionality, you get funny looks and often resentment. However, if doing your work allows you to BE more of what you are, I don't see that you have much choice.

Actors talk about learning the techniques of ''getting the job.'' Yet the best way to get a part is to let people see who you are and how you feel. If you level with casting people and producers from the beginning and express everything that is going on, at least they will know if you are what they want or not. If a person spends his life playing social roles, does anybody know who he really is? Your real power exists in your unique individuality, and in order for that to be seen, you must expose what you feel and level with yourself and the world around you.

OVERCOMING ENVY

Time is the most valuable thing we have! What we use that time for often decides our happiness and success.

How much time do you spend being envious, jealous, bitter, and angry? Many actors complain about the industry and run down other actors and their success. "She doesn't have the talent to get across the street." "His family is connected." "He hangs around with the right crowd." "She had money to start with." That whole scene is a waste of time and energy. Just remember that you never really know what went into getting a Rolls Royce, or how many dues anyone has paid. If you took the time and energy that envy consumes and put them into your own work, the results would be positive and you would be happier.

Try imagining that everyone is climbing his own mountain and that each mountain has its unique obstacles. If you can think about your journey as being unlike anyone else's, you will stop comparing yourself to others. Pick a person who has had some success and look for reasons to be happy for him. In addition to making you feel a lot better, this will stimulate your own forward thrust.

Make a list of all of your daily activities. Pick out those that waste time and replace them with productive involvement. The next time you catch yourself putting someone down or being bitter about your lot in life, ask yourself what you are accomplishing. This is the greatest country in the world and the last of the free world, and it is still possible to have anything you dream of. Anything that you can imagine is attainable if you do the right things to get it! We all have been guilty of self-sabotage. But if you look closely at a "loser," you will see how he set it up for himself.

Start admitting your problems and tendencies to sabotage, vacillate, procrastinate, and blame everyone else. Take the rap and do something to change the pattern. Habits are hard to give up, but they can be conquered. If acting is something you *must* do, then know that you have made your choice, and commit yourself to the hard work necessary to succeed. Spend your time training, growing, and being productive and soon you will find no room in your life for negative involvement. It doesn't matter what other people have, except to show us that it is also possible for us to get what we want.

THE ACTOR-AGENT RELATIONSHIP

There is an old showbiz joke about the agent who sees his client at a posh restaurant. The agent turns to a friend and says, ''Look at that SOB eating in the finest restaurants with ninety percent of my money!'' There are a lot of actor-agent stories and a great deal of friction between actors and agents. The agent-hopping game has gone on forever, and agents have forever expressed bitterness about building an actor's career only to lose him to a bigger agency when he becomes a success.

A good agent is a creative agent, a person who knows the business and how it functions. He or she reads scripts, listens to what is wanted, and sends the right actor after the part. There is nothing so demoralizing to an actor as to go on an interview for a role that is totally unsuitable. An agent who sends a whole group of clients for a role is like a painter who stands fifteen feet away from a canvas and throws a bucket of paint at it.

The actor and the agent must create a relationship with mutual respect, trust, and an understanding of each other's goals. At the very outset, the actor should know that it is he who hires the agent to work for him, not the reverse. You interview an agent for the ''job'' of representing you. He may not want to take the job, but that does not mean he is not hiring you. Finding the right agent is not easy, and you should be careful about it. Don't just add your name to a client list; be sure that the agent is interested in *you*. Find out how he sees you and what he thinks your physical essence is. Unless he is familiar with your work, make sure that he sees you perform. Any good agent will want to do that.

If, after investigating one another, you and the agent decide to give it a try, then you must be honest with him. Tell him how you feel about everything that happens between you and express your insecurities as they arise. If you walk on eggshells, a lot of resentments and misunderstandings accumulate. When that happens, it is only a matter of time until the relationship ends. If you are aware of a show being cast that you are right for, inform your agent: he can't be everywhere. There have been some legendary agent-actor relationships in this business. Sometimes an agent's unshakable faith in a client's talent has been responsible for an actor's great success. It is not easy to find or maintain a good relationship, but when you do, handle it with care!

AVOIDING THE TRAPS OF "PROFESSIONAL" PRESSURE

In order to avoid the traps that you can fall into as an actor, you must know what they are and how they happen. There are so many that it would be impossible to list them in one lesson, but here are some of the more common ones: depression, discouragement, a feeling of low self-worth.

Most actors spend a lot more time not working than they do employed. When those interminable periods mount up, you begin to question the worth of your commitment. These "crossroads" intervals are critical, and if you fall into the trap of "hanging out" at such times, the depression and apathy are compounded. What can you do to avoid that trap, or how can you pull yourself out if you are already there? The answer appears throughout this book: WORK. . . . WORK . . . WORK! If you truly want to act, then act! Start working on your instrument and craft every day; take a class; do scenes; get into a play; gather a group of your actor friends together and work on a piece of material, performing it on street corners, if necessary. Get up each morning and do exercises that eliminate your acting problems.

Some actors spend every waking hour hustling for work. They do the picture bit until they have four thousand different poses; they turn agent hopping into a career; they make a hundred telephone calls a day and convince themselves that every call brings them closer to being a star. In a way, they are better off than the actors who do nothing, except that all their energy goes toward securing employment. If they get work, they find that they are not fully prepared. What is the answer? It is to apportion your time in a proper balance between your career work and your efforts to find a job.

In my opinion the biggest acting trap relates to doing anything that is not really coming from what you feel. To avoid this pitfall you must become familiar with BEING. Discover who you are and how you feel, and learn to express that moment-to-moment life. If you deny your true impulses, you create a syndrome of denial—a chain reaction that cuts you off from the real internal life that is going on. There are other important acting traps, but this is the most important. To avoid it you must constantly look for your true feelings and express them. Set up a flow of organic life, and encourage that life to come through the lines of every scene that you do.

Another trap is the misuse of time. Actors often busy themselves with work that is counter-productive, because they lack knowledge about their craft or their instrument. Sometimes two actors rehearse a scene over and over again without really knowing what more they should be doing. They delude themselves that they can "do it" without all the effort that other profes-sionals have put into the process. I have heard hundreds of actors claim to be "naturals," gifted people who don't need training. Some even feel that to study acting would inhibit their natural gift. Nevertheless, reality always has the final word, and most of the people who in-dulge in delusion must face the truth on the stage.

Another form of delusion is the notion of *theatrical immortality*—the unfounded belief that you do not have to struggle, because your God-given gifts are so impressive that you will be sought out. This belief is comforting but foolhardy.

Tension is also a trap for actors. If it is not dealt with and eliminated each time you work, it creates problems that can follow you throughout your life. The first time that you deny the existence of your tension and try to function above it, you start on the road to suppressing your real emotional flow. The suppression becomes a conditioned response, and your talent can be buried under the tension. If you acknowledge the presence of tension, it will lose its grip on you.

Pressure is a trap that actors fall into repeatedly. On a sound stage, at the "Action" command, the pressure is on. In a sense, this is every actor's moment of truth. The tension builds, the obligation becomes monumental, and what usually happens is that the actor assumes the desired behavior, replete with natural line readings. In successive takes he repeats each line, imitating his own fraudulent intonations. This is not art! Nonetheless, it is what happens ninety percent of the time. It is bad enough when an actor doesn't know any better, but it is tragic if he knows what to do and in spite of knowing, falls prey to the pressure of the shot. You must take the time and demand your due as an artist.

Once you are in touch with what you really feel, you can work for the choice that stimulates the emotional life you wish for the scene. All the while you should include the moment-to-moment impulses that exist. If you do this under pressure, your work will be elevated from the caricature to the authentic. Pressure has many origins: wanting to be good, needing to be liked, trying to please the director, hesitating to make problems or cause too many takes, wishing to work for these people again, fearing to be considered temperamental, unprofes-sional, or "one of those Method actors." If you do succumb to fears like these, you might become the best-liked mediocre actor around. Is that why you struggle with your instrument and craft?

Next time you work in front of the camera, ask yourself, "Why am I doing this work? Who am I doing it for? What are my goals as an actor? What do I get from this, besides a paycheck? Is it worth all the years of struggle and disappointment to cop out when the pressure is applied?" It is wonderful to be liked, but more important to be respected and most important of all to respect yourself. If you walk off the studio lot feeling empty and dissatisfied, then you haven't been good to yourself. There is no greater feeling than to know you used your art and craft, no matter what anyone thinks of you. The truth is that if you are honest with yourself and loyal to your work, it accumulates in the end product—which is visible to almost everyone.

MORE THAN A DUMMY

For too many years the actor has been considered a pawn, an object to promote the writer's and/or the director's visions and theatrical concepts. Untrue! False! Unfair! We actors have allowed that to happen, and it is time to put a stop to it.

True creativity is a collaborative process. The writer creates a story filled with characters who affect each other and move the plot forward. The director contributes to the interpretation, style, and overall feeling of the piece, as well as working creatively with the actors. The actor's contribution is equally important. It is the job of a skillful and imaginative actor to create the reality of the character as written, and to bring to that organic reality the elements of his or her personality which add dimension to the writer's original concept!

The actor also stimulates emotional impulses and qualities that the writer may never have conceived of—responses that suggest complexities of emotion which the writer only vaguely alludes to and relationships that add color and depth to the character. The actor has for too long been considered a "Charley McCarthy" manipulated by the ventriloquist director. It's time you put an end to that by doing your job! In order for an actor to be creative, he must use rehearsal time fruitfully and take the necessary chances to explore choices that might lead him far afield. Stand up for your creative rights! When a director gives you a line reading, don't just take it without considering your own thoughts and feelings. Unfortunately, jobs are scarce, and our need to work for these people again makes us overly cooperative. Yet I would rather never act again than sit on the lap of a ventriloquist and let him make my mouth move. I am an *actor,* not a dummy!

COMMUNICATING WITH THE DIRECTOR

There are not many places where a director can receive good training, and most directors, whether they work in the theatre or in films, have almost no understanding of an organic process of acting. They direct in "result" terms, meaning that they ask the actor to deliver an emotional response without any further involvement with that actor's process. This is fine for an actor who has a well-developed craft and knows what he is doing. Even so, however, no relationship develops between the director and the actor. Creating is a collaborative experience, and when there is no collaboration, the level of the work deteriorates.

What are the alternatives? Do we create schools for directors that teach them to be sensitive to actors' problems? Or do we enforce the rigid line between director and actor and continue to wage a polite war, in which the actors listen to what he says and then do what they want to? That is a "no win" situation. Everybody wants essentially the same thing: to do good work and fulfill the material. So why not work together instead of separately?

The actor's obligation in this relationship is to help the director to direct him. You don't go to a doctor and make him guess what is wrong with you. do you? Most people are very private about themselves, particularly to strangers. When you work in television or on a film, you may meet your director for the first time when you come to work. You sometimes feel tense and insecure in this new situation, so you remain polite and quiet and try to do what is asked of you. That is not an atmosphere of creativity! Let your director know how you feel, and find out something about him. Ask him how he sees the scene; get an idea of what he wants. *Communicate!* As you rehearse, continue to help the director to direct you. Share your immediate problems, and give him some idea of what he can do to affect you in the area that he wants. Tell him that you need time to work with your choices. There are no awards for "fast" actors, only good ones! Ask as many questions as you need to, because you are an important component in this experience. You will be surprised to see that when you involve a director in this kind of collaboration, he usually responds with interest and excitement.

It is important to be able to perceive where a director is in his understanding of the creative process. Out of pure ignorance, some directors feel hostile to Method actors. They don't even know what a Method actor is, but they don't want to deal with them. Watch the way your director works with the other actors to know how to approach him and get the very best from him. Remember that it is not a contest between the two of you, but a collaboration that might lead to a special result. Never underestimate anyone! No matter what you think of your director, he has eyes and can see you on a level of objectivity that you do not have in relation to yourself.

HOW TO GET COOPERATION FROM OTHER ACTORS

"How can you prepare to do a scene with another actor who is off in a corner reading the *Hollywood Reporter* and drinking coffee?"

"What do you do when the people around you, including the director, are amused by the way you are working?"

"How do you deal with an actor who won't get involved with you?"

"Have you ever done a scene with an actor who is serious enough about the work, but not equipped to do any more than stare at your chin when he acts?"

To all these exasperated questions, the answer is that you *can* work with such actors, though it certainly makes your job more difficult. There are many ways to use the other actor without his knowing that you are doing so. Before you start the scene, you can involve him in normal conversation, weaving in some of your choices and slowly establishing an involvement with him.

Selective Emphasis
Suppose that the scene you are going to do involves admiration: your character is in awe of the other character and has spent years admiring his accomplishments. Instead of preparing alone, you might engage the other actor in conversation, selectively emphasizing all his attributes that you respect and admire. You progressively involve the other actor with your "improvisation" until he is responding somewhat the way his character does in the scene. If he takes what you are saying personally, and most people do when they are not "acting," he should behave much as the character would.

Trick the Other Actor

When you are actually filming a scene and the other actor is not relating, you can force contact by following the actor's eyes until he must relate to you. Or you can do something unexpected that he will impulsively respond to. However, if you do trick the other actor, be prepared to carry the ball, since it might disorient him and cause him to lose his lines. Some of the most exciting work I have ever seen has come from moments like this. Naturally you have a responsibility to do your work, to be professional, and to say the words as written! In that framework the larger responsibility is to be real, and reality is something you must create. In an instance like this you have accomplished many things. First, you are both really involved with each other, and secondly, you have established a foundation for the scene. You have a beginning to a relationship, and in most cases it will carry into the scene. When I tell people to do something like this, they often say that it is deception. Well, maybe it is! I would rather be a deceptive artist than a truthful faker!

Appeal for Help

Another way to get an actor to prepare with you is to appeal to him for help. Tell him that you would like to prepare for the scene, and ask if he will help you to do a few things. When you approach another actor like that, you disobligate him from doing "those classroom things," and usually he does it for you! All the while, you both benefit by it.

HELP YOURSELF WITH CHARTS

Let us suppose that you have gotten a big part in a movie and that you have done all the preparation. Your instrument is primed and ready to work, you have gone through the script many times, and you have made some choices that seem to affect you the way you want to be affected. What is the next step in the process? Make two charts: a *continuity* chart and a *choice and obligation* chart.

Continuity Chart

The continuity chart helps you follow the emotional flow of your character through the script. Since most films are shot out of sequence, it is necessary to know what the emotional life was in each scene so that you can re-create this base before you work for your choices in subsequent scenes. Start with the first scene you are in and describe the emotional content of the scene, the relationship elements, and any other pertinent information that would help you. Make notes on how each scene affects the life of the following scene, and what the emotional springboards are. This chart will help you to create the appropriate impulses and emotions, so that even when you shoot a scene which is supposed to immediately follow a scene you shot five days ago, it will make sense.

Choice and Obligation Chart

Draw a line in the center of a piece of typing paper. On the left side describe the emotional obligations of the scene, the character's feelings, and the character's motivation. Clearly identify all the emotional elements in the scene. On the right side of the sheet list all the possible choices and choice approaches in order of their importance. With this chart you are always aware of the content of every scene and the specific choices that you have decided to try.

No matter where you are or what is being done, you can always refer to your charts to find what the obligations are and what you are going to do to fulfill them. Of course, you are not bound to any of the choices you have made; you can modify or completely change them. The charts are like a navigational map that tells you where you have been, where you are going, and what is the best route for getting there. Start using these charts in your scene work, your acting class, or your workshop. Keep your charts with you when you rehearse, since it helps you to make a better use of your time. After using them for a while you won't want to be without them. If you make notes in the margin as to how each choice affected you, they will become good references for future scenes. Keep all your charts for a complete repertoire of choices that you have explored and how they affected you.

PUTTING IT ALL TOGETHER

It is important to act all the time and to do scene work consistently. The pressures of time, tension, the obligation to be good, and the wish to please get in the way of the work! When the director says "Action!" the pressure is on, and a lot of the time, actors forget the work and "get through" the take. There is a kind of tension in the atmosphere, and you can be infected by it.

What works best for me is to admit any tension or anxiety, then to do a Personal Inventory, finding out how I feel on a moment-to-moment basis and trying to express those impulses. Next I look around the set and try to become selflessly involved in everyone I see by doing an Observe, Wonder, and Perceive exercise. After doing all these, I start to work for the choice that I think will stimulate the behavior I want to experience.

If you have to worry about lines, you will very likely short-circuit your whole creative process. Everything you do on the set is for the purpose of fulfilling your responsibilities to the role. Be careful not to waste precious time with small talk.

Since a film is almost always shot out of continuity, you should make a shot list for yourself, describing everything that happens in each scene and how it is affected by the scenes before and after it. By doing that, you will always know what the emotional life of the character was before the scene you are about to do. Then you can choose the proper preparation for the scene at hand.

Avoid listening to yourself and repeating a line the identical way you did in the last take because it sounded good. Make sure you do your homework. Don't come to the set and "wing it," because there are no miracles!

An actor prepares and prepares and prepares! If you have a craft and get into trouble, go to your craft and it will get you out of that trouble. Work for reality, not approval. You know when what you are doing feels right, and you know when it doesn't.

This is my one and only life.
If I am not for me, then who will be?

NOTES

NOTES

NOTES

NOTES

NOTES

NOTES

NOTES

NOTES

NOTES

NOTES

If you found the information in this book valuable, you'll be interested to know that cassette tapes by Eric Morris are now available. These 60- and 90-minute audio tapes were recorded live at actual workshops and seminars conducted by Mr. Morris and are ideal for use in conjunction with his books *Being and Doing* and *No Acting Please*. The tapes are offered in a series covering the entire system of work, but each separate tape is a complete and exciting learning tool by itself.

To receive the first tape plus a full information brochure, send your check for $5.95 plus $1.00 for postage and handling to:

Whitehouse/Spelling Publications
8004 Fareholm Drive
Los Angeles, California 90046

Money refunded if not satisfied.